THE TUPPER LECTURES
ON SHAKESPEARE
Sponsored by
THE GEORGE WASHINGTON UNIVERSITY

SHAKESPEARE'S
CRAFT | *Eight Lectures*

Edited, with an Introduction by
PHILIP H. HIGHFILL, JR.

Published for
THE GEORGE WASHINGTON UNIVERSITY
by
SOUTHERN ILLINOIS UNIVERSITY PRESS
Carbondale and Edwardsville

COPYRIGHT © 1982
BY THE GEORGE WASHINGTON UNIVERSITY
All rights reserved
Printed in the United States of America
Edited by Beatrice R. Moore

Library of Congress Cataloging in Publication Data

Main entry under title:

Shakespeare's craft.

(The Tupper lectures on Shakespeare)
Contents: Irony and its interrelatedness in
Shakespeare / David Bevington — Julius Caesar
and Coriolanus / Anne Barton — Two scenes from
Macbeth / Harry Levin — [etc.]
   1. Shakespeare, William, 1564–1616—Criticism
and interpretation—Addresses, essays, lectures.
I. Highfill Philip H. II. Series.
PR2976.S339   822.3′3   81–9386
ISBN 0–8093–1014–7   AACR2

Contents

Introduction

Like any other art, fine teaching is mysterious in its causes. Unlike some others, its excellence cannot be estimated at once but can be seen only in its lasting effects. Members of several generations of students of the late Fred Salisbury Tupper continue to give testimony of his extraordinary success as a teacher of Shakespeare, joining enthusiastically with his colleagues and other friends in support of the series of annual lectures which commemorate his services.

The Tupper Lectures were inaugurated in 1965. They first assumed printed form in *Shakespeare's Art*, the volume of essays edited by Milton Crane in 1973. The essays in this second collection go to press just as we prepare to hear the latest of the notable Shakespeareans who come each spring to The George Washington University to share their critical perceptions and scholarly discoveries. Professor Crane has described the difficulties which confront those who are invited to participate in the series: the need to engage the interests of veteran specialists, young students, and nonspecialists among the interested public and to hold the attention of an audience with words that can "pass equally well the critical scrutiny reserved for the printed page." Like their predecessors, our essayists of the present volume have splendidly satisfied those exacting requirements.

The stimulating variety which characterized the first collection of essays is also one of the attractions of this second series. David Bevington, in "Irony and its Interrelatedness in Shakespeare," ranges confidently through a dozen plays in discovering "the technical links between verbal irony, dramatic irony, and the larger irony that is both a criticism of life and a principle of dramatic structure." Anne Barton, in "*Julius Caesar* and *Coriolanus*: Shakespeare's Roman World of Words," takes us to Rome for a fresh inspection of the social effects of public utterance, the subtly sinister or quietly beneficent results of demagogic suasion. In "Two Scenes from *Macbeth*," Harry Levin deepens our understanding of the theological and thematic significances and psychological intricacies of the porter's response to the portentous knocking at the gate and of the "slumbering agitation" of Lady Macbeth's somnambulism. Hallett Smith ushers us on an excursion through "The Poetry of the Lyric Group: *Richard II*, *Romeo and Juliet*, *A Midsummer Night's Dream*," examining the contributions of melody and imagery to dramatic effect.

Robert B. Heilman wittily investigates modes of relationship between farce and comedy in "Shakespeare's Variations on Farcical Style" and points to the "variegated employment of farce" even in some "serious" plays. Eugene Waith's "Shakespeare and the Ceremonies of Romance" demonstrates the use of epic and romance traditions of religious ceremony and the influence of suggestions from earlier drama in the ceremonial scenes of *The Winter's Tale*, *Cymbeline*, *The Two Noble Kinsmen* and *Henry VIII*. In "Shakespeare's Stage Audiences: The Playwright's Reflections and Control of Audience Response," Alvin B. Kernan interprets for us evidence regarding the character of the sixteenth-century playgoer which he finds in five plays-within-the-play. Finally, in "Looking for Shakespeare," Samuel Schoenbaum begins with a retrospection of his "long obsessive-compulsive pursuit" of Shakespearean records and relics, touches on Shakespearean forgery, and ends whimsically but persuasively in a comparison of *King Lear* to the film *Harry and Tonto*.

PHILIP H. HIGHFILL, JR.

Irony and Its Interrelatedness in Shakespeare 1

DAVID BEVINGTON

My purpose is to study the interrelation of various kinds of
irony in Shakespeare—first of all, irony of speech or verbal
irony, second, dramatic irony in which the audience per-
ceives truths concealed from various characters on stage,
and third a more embracing irony which is both a criticism
of life and a principle of dramatic structure, one in which
the outcome of events differs incongruously from the expected result. I should like to differentiate these various
kinds of irony in Shakespeare and at the same time attempt
to show their interrelatedness and their mutual dependency
on a consistent authorial point of view. Lastly, I should like
to concentrate on the last and largest of these categories of
irony and suggest ways in which patterns of ironic viewpoint can be used to differentiate genres—that is, I propose
to find a characteristic handling of irony in the Roman or
classical tragedies, another in the tragedies that are not Roman or classical, and still another in the late tragicomic romances.

To begin with, then, let us ask if the term irony as applied
in these three senses—verbal irony, dramatic irony, and
irony as both a criticism of life and a principle of dramatic
structure—can be said to share a common meaning. Historically, as a number of students of irony have shown,[1] the
term *eironeia* is first used in the comedies of Aristophanes

1. See especially J. A. K. Thompson, *Irony: An Historical Introduc-
tion* (Cambridge, Mass.: Harvard University Press, 1927), Alan L.
Thompson, *The Dry Mock: A Study of Irony in Drama* (Berkeley and Los
Angeles: University of California Press, 1948), G. G. Sedgwick, *Of Irony
Especially in Drama* (Toronto: University of Toronto Press, 1948),
Bert O. States, *Irony and Drama: A Poetics* (Ithaca: Cornell University

and then in Aristotle as a word meaning litotes or under-statement, a tendency toward telling less than the whole truth in contrast to *alazoneia* or boastful overstatement. Irony in this sense is supremely illustrated by Socrates' role in the dialogues of Plato: the philosopher habitually pre-tends to be an inexperienced person in order to mock and deflate the pompous learning of his Sophist opponents. From its inception, then, the term irony implied a broad philosophical perspective rather than simply a mode of speech. Yet in the hands of the classical rhetoricians such as Cicero and Quintilian, the term acquired a primary meaning as a rhetorical trope, one in which the speaker's words carry the opposite meaning of his actual intent. This narrowed technical meaning generally prevailed as a definition throughout the Middle Ages and Renaissance and was per-haps codified in this sense by Puttenham's apt phrase for verbal irony as a "dry mock."[2]

Not until the Romantic era of Tieck, Friedrich Schlegel, and the English Bishop Connop Thirlwall (1833), in fact, did irony begin again to take on broader meaning. Once the search for a broader significance began, it led to such enthu-siastic excesses that it has generated in modern times a backlash against Romantic tendencies to rhapsodize. Schle-gel's view of irony as "transzendentale Buffonerie," as "joy in the possession of an infinite mind," and as spiritual free-dom and detachment, as well as Goethe's invocation of irony as "die hohe Lebensansicht," have produced among others the famous attack by Irving Babbitt in his *Rousseau and Romanticism* (1919).[3] Tieck's fondness for seeing Shakespeare as an ironist in everything he wrote has led to a commendable caution about using the term so indiscrimi-nately. Bishop Thirlwall's formulation of the concept of dra-matic irony (or "practical irony," as he called it) has proved useful to modern criticism, but it has been pointed out that the Greeks never used the term in this sense despite the fact

Press, 1971), and Robert B. Sharpe, *Irony in the Drama* (Chapel Hill: University of North Carolina Press, 1959).

2. From Puttenham's *Arte of English Poesie*, 1589. See David Worces-ter, *The Art of Satire* (Cambridge, Mass.: Harvard University Press, 1940), p. 78.

3. See Sedgwick, *Of Irony*, pp. 15–17.

that the plays of Sophocles and Euripides often brilliantly exemplify the technique we now call dramatic irony. The welter of definitions proposed since the early nineteenth century has prompted some modern students of irony, such as Wayne Booth,[4] to wish that some term other than irony could be found for the broader and sometimes vaguer senses in which it is so often employed. H. W. Fowler, in his *Dictionary of Modern English Usage*, warns that the phrase "irony of fate" is now to be classed "as a Hackneyed Phrase," and is even to be placed ignominiously on the "retired list of clichés."[5] Several recent studies of irony find it necessary to conclude with a cautionary chapter on the limits of the term.[6]

Despite the risks involved in discussing irony as a comprehensive view of man's fate, I should like to argue that the generally understood meaning of irony today, even the hackneyed sense deplored by Fowler, is neither too vague nor too broad to be applied to Shakespeare and specifically related to his use of the more concrete forms of irony, verbal irony and dramatic irony. As J. A. K. Thomson has wisely said, irony as a criticism of life is as hard to define as is poetry but perhaps no harder to recognize.[7] As applied today to drama or indeed to any fictional or real-life situation, this kind of irony has to do with life's incongruities: things seldom work out as planned. Fate constantly amuses herself at our expense, and those of us who are witty enough to perceive the incongruities defend ourselves by joining in ironic laughter. In this sense we say it is ironic that the medieval Catholic Church, after having done its best to abolish drama throughout the fifth-century Roman empire because of its lewd tendencies, nevertheless gave birth during the tenth century to drama as a part of the Church's own liturgy. Or, we say, how ironic that Beethoven, one of the greatest composers of all time, should have suffered from total deafness—so much so that he is reported to have practiced on a

4. Wayne C. Booth, *A Rhetoric of Irony* (Chicago: University of Chicago Press, 1974).

5. As quoted in Sedgwick, *Of Irony*, p. 7.

6. See especially States, *Irony and Drama*, chap. 10, and Thompson, *The Dry Mock*, chap. 10.

7. Thomson, *Irony*, p. 1.

stringed instrument that was always excruciatingly out of tune and to have pounded away at a piano that gradually lost all of its strings until it became, like Beethoven's own sense of hearing, utterly without sound. In an ironic vision of this sort, man is blind to his own destiny; forces beyond his control seem to play with him in sport. Such a view is often detached and wryly humorous. The term "irony" in this sense often implies a controlled acceptance of life's incongruities as something unavoidable, a reality with which man has to come to terms. The emotional range accompanying such an acceptance can vary from tranquil affirmation to bitterness, but the motivation of the ironic response remains essentially the same: a defensive challenge of seemingly unavoidable destiny through a comic though often painful perception of the absurdities contained in that destiny. As with the ancient Greeks, we find in the term *eironeia* considerably more than a simple figure of speech.

What, however, are the technical links between verbal irony, dramatic irony, and the larger irony that is both a criticism of life and a principle of dramatic structure? In what sense can they be said to operate through similar mechanisms and elicit comparable emotional and intellectual responses? Let me begin with an example from *A Midsummer Night's Dream*, commenting first on verbal irony as a way of speech.

It is not always easy to distinguish between simple ironic statement and dramatic irony. Since we are dealing in this analysis with plays entirely, we must always of course postulate the presence of an audience and must take the audience into account in determining the force and significance of an ironic statement. Whenever an ironic statement is made on the stage in the presence of another character, the audience in a sense inevitably knows something that one or more characters on stage do not know, and to that extent dramatic irony is at work. Irony, in fact, always depends on a double audience, as Fowler points out.[8] There must always be present those on the one hand who fail to understand the true intent of the speaker's ironic statement or the

8. H. W. Fowler, *A Dictionary of Modern English Usage* (Oxford: Clarendon Press, 1926, 1952), p. 295.

unspoken irony of the situation, and on the other hand those
who understand the ironic intention of the speaker and who
therefore share in common a wisdom superior to those who
fail to comprehend. Still, we can talk about ironic statement
in a play that would be ironic even if an audience were not
present or were present only in the sense in which an audience is also present in the reading of a novel or short story.
We as audience merely overhear an ironic statement directed at some other character on stage. Examples are to be
found in profusion in the final act of *A Midsummer Night's
Dream*, when Duke Theseus, Queen Hippolyta, and the
lords and ladies of the court are gathered on stage to witness
a performance of "Pyramus and Thisbe" by Bottom the
Weaver and his fellow Thespians. When Snout the Tinker
explains to his noble spectators that he is to present a wall
in their interlude, and is for that reason adorned with lime,
hair, and a crannied hole or chink, through which the lovers
are to whisper, his naïve impersonation calls forth witty
observations from the amused onlookers. "Would you desire lime and hair to speak better?" asks Theseus, and Demetrius answers in kind: "It is the wittiest partition that ever
I heard discourse, my lord." This is ironic statement, since
Demetrius means just the opposite: this is the stupidest stuff
he has ever heard, though I suppose in a technical sense it
is the wittiest *partition* he has heard since he has never
heard a partition before. Theseus' statement is a good example of an ironic question, clearly implying the sort of
answer that Demetrius gives—so clearly implying that answer, in fact, that Demetrius' spelling out the obvious loses
some of the potential wit.

Several things are happening here at once, then. On its
surface, the exchange of ironic statements between Theseus
and Demetrius forges a bond of understanding between
them at the expense of a gull, or butt—i.e., Snout the
Tinker and his fellow tradesmen. Theseus' question implies
a lofty superiority to the naïve kind of playacting the courtiers are witnessing, a superiority that will be recognized by
all thoughtful cultivated men. The ironic form of the question is a test to discriminate those who perceive the ridicu-
lousness of the situation from those who don't. Demetrius,

as a young courtier, is anxious to prove that he belongs to the courtly set and can see the purpose in Theseus' remarks.

At the same time, we as audience are present, and we may sense something not entirely attractive in Demetrius' eagerness to chime in with Theseus' scoffing. We may in fact ultimately become a little uneasy about the unfeeling wit of all the court party, especially when the ironic remarks at the expense of poor "Pyramus and Thisbe" begin to pile on top of one another: "Well roared, lion!" "Well run, Thisbe!" or "No epilogue, I pray you, for your play needs no excuse." We are not perfect sharers, in other words, in the smugly ironic community formed by the court party. Instead, we are distanced from them. We sense that Theseus' genteel and wry dismissal of all illusion as mere madness (since, he insists, the poet, the madman, and the lover are "of imagination all compact") is too limited a view to encompass all that has happened in the larger play of which he too is a part. Theseus undergoes no transforming experience in the forest; he is one who "never may believe / These antique fables, nor these fairy toys."

At this point, the play as a whole gently but ironically mocks Theseus for dwelling too exclusively in the realm of the tangible world. This is a dramatic irony since it is shared among the spectators of *A Midsummer Night's Dream* at the expense of certain characters on stage. We know, or think we know, what Theseus cannot see, that the fairies are as "real" as he is in the world of Shakespeare's play. We share an interpretation with others who respond as we do and with the author, if we interpret him correctly. (Proving his intent is of course problematical; what we really do is to postulate an authorial position with which we agree and then congratulate ourselves for seeing things in as sophisticated a way as the author did.) The dramatic irony we enjoy, mildly at the expense of Theseus (who remains, after all, an admirable character), both embraces and qualifies the ironies of statement shared by Theseus and his friends at the expense of Bottom and company.

Finally, we come to the most embracing irony of the play, irony both as a criticism of life and as a structuring device for the play as a whole. It is best expressed in the final words of Puck, who turns the whole play into a dream or vision no more real than the play of "Pyramus and Thisbe": "Think but this, and all is mended, / That you have but slumber'd here / While these visions did appear." At this point, the gentle ironies of the play, focusing repeatedly on man's capacity for humorously fatuous self-deception, are broadened to include those of us who are watching. No one is spared, not even the author himself, since he insists that his play is nothing more than illusion. This, I take it, is an example of Kierkegaard's observation on irony in Shakespeare, when he argues that irony becomes so pervasive and omnipresent in Shakespeare's work that "the visible irony in the poem is in turn ironically mastered."[9]

Other instances of verbal irony in Shakespeare's plays similarly are closely tied to a larger framework of dramatic irony, in which we as audience appreciate something not apparent to characters on stage, and to a still larger framework of irony as a structuring principle and device of viewpoint. Take, for example, the fourth scene in act V of *1 Henry VI*, in which Richard Plantagenet the Duke of York and the Earl of Warwick, leading the English armies in France, take into custody the infamous Joan of Arc. Joan is a character who invites a withering sort of irony in Shakespeare's play; she was regarded by the English of Shakespeare's time as a witch and a whore in man's clothing. Earlier in the play, Lord Talbot has referred contemptuously to Joan as "the Dauphin's grace, / His new-come champion, virtuous Joan of Arc" (II, ii, 20). This is irony of the most obvious sort and hence of the widest possible appeal, the least likely to be taken literally—at least among English audiences. Equally obvious, for the same reasons, are York's and Warwick's incredulous responses to Joan's assertion that she is pregnant and therefore ought not to be executed. "Now heaven forfend!" exclaims York with mock piety, "the holy maid with child!" Warwick chimes in with more spurious religiosity: "The greatest miracle that e'er ye wrought!" (V,iv, 65–66). The joke is based in part on the blasphemous association of Joan with the Virgin Mary, an association that

9. Søren Kierkegaard, *The Concept of Irony*, trans. Lee M. Capel (London: Collins, 1966), p. 336.

runs throughout the play and is fostered to no small degree by Joan herself. As York derisively chants, "And yet, forsooth, she is a virgin pure."

This, as I said, is ironic statement of the most obvious sort possible. No Englishman in Shakespeare's audience could possibly have missed the joke. The audience and all the English characters on stage join forces in a community of satirical laughter at the expense of the effete French and their wanton, spell-practicing woman-general. The laughter is surely increased, as Leslie Fiedler argues,[10] by a widely felt attitude of hostility toward the type of dominating, emasculating woman, one who usurps the male's role and his attire. York and Warwick are at pains to prove, like Lord Talbot earlier in the play, that they cannot be seduced by this Circean, Amazonian witch. Nevertheless, a dramatic irony is readily apparent as well. It is one thing to have the admirable Lord Talbot use satirical language about Joan earlier in the play; it is quite another to hear the scheming Richard Plantagenet of York use the same abusive language in V, iv. The very similarity of roles vis-à-vis Joan accentuates the contrast in motive. York has replaced Talbot as general in France and as nemesis of Joan, but for distressingly different reasons. We as audience know that York is ultimately aiming at the subversion of political order, whereas Talbot was defending the English throne and its rightful territories. This knowledge of York's villainy distances us from that community of sympathy created by his ironic statements concerning Joan. And this dramatic irony which we perceive operates in much the same ways as verbal irony: York's words do not mean to us what they seem to say, because we know that his perverse intentions are in fact the very opposite of his patriotic stance. Two groups of listeners respond to York's speeches: those on stage who are deceived by his stratagems, and we in the audience who perceive an incongruous intent. Dramatic irony therefore works like irony of statement in forming a community of those who perceive the gap between appearance and reality at the expense of those who do not. Yet the knowledgeable commu-

10. Leslie A. Fiedler, *The Stranger in Shakespeare* (New York: Stein and Day, 1972), pp. 52–53, 56–63.

nity that understands York's true political intent is a significantly smaller group than that which understands his more obvious verbal irony directed at Joan; and the disparity between these two levels of comprehension is itself a source of irony. We as audience share with one another a foreboding that the seemingly happy patriotic moment of Joan's capture is burdened with an imminent prospect of England's failure in France. The keenest irony, perhaps, is that York is more like Joan than he is unlike her: both are types of disorder and dissension.

To consider finally and briefly the largest sort of irony in *1 Henry VI*, that of an overall structural pattern, we need only consider the recurring emblem of the domineering female.[11] Although Talbot resists the charms of both Joan and the Countess of Auvergne, weaker men yield again and again to Amazonian women: the Dauphin Charles to Joan, Burgundy to Joan, Suffolk to Margaret, and—finally and most ominously—King Henry to Margaret as well. The play ends on this note of submission of reason to will.

Sometimes ironic statement in Shakespeare's plays is properly understood chiefly by the audience and is at the expense of virtually all characters on stage other than the person who is speaking. In such instances, the ironic statement is apt to be choric in effect and is thus especially closely tied to a perception of the play's overall ironic pattern. An example of this sort can be found in *King John*, act II, when King John of England and King Philip of France meet before the gates of Angiers. Both kings lay claim to Angiers as part of their rightful territories. The citizens of Angiers circumspectly decide, under these circumstances, to open their gates to "the king of England"—but only when John and Philip have decided between themselves who is possessor of that contested title. John and Philip are about to come to blows in order to resolve their dispute, when the Bastard Philip cannily suggests that they unite until they have jointly overwhelmed Angiers; afterward, they can quarrel among themselves. The two kings are delighted with this counsel of "policy" and resolve to attack Angiers

11. David Bevington, "The Domineering Female in 1 Henry VI," *Shakespeare Studies* 2 (1966): 51–58.

in concert: John from the west, Philip from the south, and
Limoges of Austria (the third ally) from the north. From
these various directions, they say, they will "rain their drift
of bullets on this town" (II, i, 412). What we are interested
in is the Bastard's choric comment on the plot he has thus
set in motion. "O prudent discipline!" he exults, "From
north to south, / Austria and France shoot in each other's
mouth. / I'll stir them to it." This remark could of course be
directed partly at King John, who will profit from any
scheme that points France's and Austria's guns at one another. We react to the statement in part, however, as choric
and as expressive of the larger ironies inherent in this scene
and this play. The universal political situation as we perceive it through the Bastard's eyes is one of "commodity."
King Philip is persuaded one moment to fight the English in
defense of his territorial claims, then forms a marriage alli-
ance with England when he is offered a handsome enough
dowry, and finally turns against England once again at the
self-interested promptings of the Roman church. The citizens of Angiers are prepared to accommodate themselves to
the winning side in the power-struggle, whichever side that
happens to be. Even John's claims to his own throne are
justified by mere expediency, by *de facto* rule. *Realpolitik*
underlies every political relationship, and the Bastard's ex-
ulting response is to turn Machiavellism into a game. He
can persuade France and England to fight temporarily on the
same side, or he can hoodwink France and Austria into aiming their guns at one another, all in the name of "commodity." Hence, his ironic statement, "O prudent discipline!" simply translates into choric form an irony which we
perceive along with the Bastard. We share with him a view
of the wryly comic absurdity of the world's universal pen-
chant for self-serving games of policy, and we take pleasure
in his way of giving verbal expression to this view through
the rhetorical figure of irony. He and we share the superior
position of knowing why his statement, "O prudent discipline," means the very opposite of what he purports to say.

More examples of this sort of ironic statement giving
choric expression to a broadly based irony of situation could
be discussed in *Hamlet*, in such utterances as "This is most

brave" (addressed by Hamlet to himself in a frenzy of self-accusation for his inability to act), or "Sir, I lack advancement." This later statement is addressed to Rosencrantz, who characteristically thinks he can explain Hamlet's purported madness in political terms and who therefore is completely taken in by Hamlet's ironic explanation, "Sir, I lack advancement." "How can that be," Rosencrantz rejoins, "when you have the voice of / the King himself for your succession in Denmark?" (III, ii, 338–41). In other words, Rosencrantz takes straight an answer that Hamlet had meant as mock of Rosencrantz' simpleminded search for an explanation of mad behavior. There is nothing quite so gratifying to an ironist as to induce someone to react seriously to ironic statement and thereby demonstrate his lack of perception.

Rather than pursue these instances in detail, however, I should like to turn to the use of double entendre as a form of verbal irony. The effect is often far from choric; although we perceive the irony and delight in its wit, we also perceive that double entendre is frequently used as a cruel weapon by persons whose actions fill us with dismay or revulsion.[12] Rather than being choric, therefore, double entendres are usually laden with dramatic irony (distancing us from the characters on stage) and are used as devices of anticipation, prophecy, or structuring of the play. This use of irony illustrates William Empson's observation that irony is an intelligible way of reminding the audience of the rest of the play while seeing a single part of it.[13] Double entendre as ironic statement is particularly abundant in the play of *Richard III*. Richard himself loves quibbles that convey a sinister meaning unknown to his intended victims. To his brother Clarence, for example, in the first scene, Richard offers the following ostensible assurance of concern for his unjust imprisonment: "Well, your imprisonment shall not be long; / I will deliver you, or else lie for you" (I, i, 115). In truth, Clarence's imprisonment will not last long, for we have already been told by Richard of his plan to do away

12. See Robert Y. Turner, *Shakespeare's Apprenticeship* (Chicago: University of Chicago Press, 1974), chap. 5.

13. William Empson, *English Pastoral Poetry* (New York: W. W. Norton, 1938), chap. 3. See also States, *Irony and Drama*, p. 28.

with Clarence this very day. The word "lie" is a grisly pun, meaning to "lie in prison in your stead" and also to "tell lies, betray." The same sinister joking informs Richard's speculation that Clarence will be "new-christen'd in the Tower." Richard gloats to the audience about his ability to deceive thus with words. When in act III, scene i he disguises with double meaning a threat upon the life of young Prince Edward, Richard goes on to say in an aside: "Thus, like the formal vice, Iniquity, / I moralize two meanings in one word" (82–83). The device is recognizably a stage convention derived from the morality play.

The device is used not only by Richard but by his henchmen, Catesby and Buckingham. When, for example, Catesby interviews the Lord Hastings at Richard's request and finds the Lord Chamberlain unwilling to go along with Richard's scheme to have himself crowned rather than young Prince Edward, Catesby reassures Hastings of his rising political favor in the eyes of Richard and Buckingham. "The princes both make high account of you," he says to Hastings, and then adds in an aside for our delectation: "For they account his head upon the bridge" (III, ii, 69–70). Thus the pun as a rhetorical figure—in this instance a pun on the words "account" and "high"—doubles as ironic statement in which the speaker explains privately to the audience that his original statement actually meant the opposite of what it seemed to say.

Later in the same scene, Buckingham offers a series of similar ironic double entendres as he and Lord Hastings journey together to the Tower—the Tower from which, plainly, Hastings will never return. Part of the irony is that Hastings is at this very moment celebrating the capture and execution by Richard's command of Hastings' political enemies, the Queen's kindred. Surely the man who has prevailed over Rivers, Grey, and Dorset must be a friend on whom Hastings can rely. Part of the irony too is that Hastings happens to encounter a priest at this moment when, although he doesn't yet know it, he is in need of extreme unction. Buckingham seizes upon the ironic circumstance in such a way as to remind us continually of the underlying grim humor of the situation. "What, talking with a priest,

Lord Chamberlain?" Buckingham rallies Hastings. "Your friends at Pomfret, they do need the priest; / Your honor hath no shriving work in hand." Hastings' answer unintentionally links the forthcoming circumstances of his own death with those of the Queen's kindred, though he himself cannot of course be expected to grasp the ironic meaning. "Good faith," he replies, "and when I met this holy man, / The men you talk of came into my mind. / What, go you toward the Tower?" / "I do, my lord," answers Buckingham, "but long I cannot stay there. / I shall return before your lordship thence." To which Hastings replies, "Nay, like enough, for I stay dinner there." Buckingham, aside: "And supper too, although thou know'st it not." And the irony continues on into the council scene held inside the Tower.

This use of double entendre as ironic statement has quite a different impact than that of the Bastard Philip's choric observations about "prudent discipline" or Hamlet's wry jest about lacking advancement. Those latter statements originate from a sympathetic bond between us and the speaker that is lacking in the case of Richard III and his henchmen. To be sure, we are in on Richard's joke, and we admire his adroitness; to that important extent the irony works as it always does, forging a community of those who see the humorous discrepancy between appearance and reality at the expense of those who do not. Nevertheless, we disapprove morally of Richard's acts and are far more apt to sympathize with his victims even though we recognize that they are partly to blame for their own impending downfalls. Accordingly, we are distanced from the ironist on stage and regard his comic viewpoint as only one dramatic ingredient in the larger framework of the play. Indeed, we belatedly perceive an ironic pattern in *Richard III* of which the protagonist himself is totally unaware until too late, a pattern that will call Richard to account for his crimes and lead him to his destruction much as he has led the other characters to their untimely but often deserved ends. What we must next examine, then, is the interplay between a grim irony controlled by a manipulating character like Richard and a larger irony in which the schemer is himself outdone by his own villainy and by a benign overseeing cosmic force.

The archetype of this doubly ironic vision is the story of the devil's futile attempts to entrap Christ, especially as seen through the eyes of medieval and apocryphal legend. A good name for the archetypal story is "the beguiler beguiled."[14] One version of it, found for example in the York and N Town Passion sequences, sees the devil as a figure whose own cleverness brings about his downfall. Because the devil disobeyed God and then deceived Adam and Eve, he deserves to be outwitted and outmaneuvered by Christ. The Incarnation, giving human form to Christ, is a device to conceal Christ's true identity from the devil; in the scene of the temptation in the wilderness, we see plainly that the devil does not know that his adversary is God himself. Accordingly, the devil plots to kill his adversary and finds an apt agent in Judas Iscariot. Everything goes along as planned through the arrest and betrayal; what could be more humiliating and defeating to the cause of goodness than to have Christ hanged like a common thief?

Suddenly, however, and much too late, the devil realizes that by precipitating the crucifixion of the son of God he has set in motion the salvation of the human race. Curses, foiled! Frantically, the devil attempts to stop his own show by appearing to Pilate's wife in a dream, urging her for her own safety and that of her husband to prevent the crucifixion and set Christ free. (This is in fact the N Town dramatist's way of motivating Pilate's reluctance to allow Christ to be executed.) Of course it is too late: Christ is crucified and descends into hell—where we see another fine ironic scene in which the devils torment one another for their own stupidity in having allowed this ridiculous situation to develop. Proverbially, the beguiler has been beguiled. The devil plays the *alazon* to Christ's role as *eiron*. This reading of the Passion story as a contest of guile is derived in part from 1 Corinthians 2:7–8, where St. Paul writes: "I speak of God's hidden wisdom, his secret purpose framed from

14. On the beguiler beguiled, see Alan Nelson, "The Contest of Guile in the Middle English Corpus Christi Play." (Ph.D. diss., University of California, Berkeley, 1966). The motif of Pilate's wife's dream is of course much older than the Corpus Christi cycle, and is to be found in the Passion play from Monte Cassino in the twelfth century.

the very beginning to bring us to our full glory. The powers that rule the world have never known it; if they had, they would not have crucified the Lord of Glory."

Richard III's career follows a similar course. At first, the schemer appears to be masterfully in control of all those around him. His bravura acts of disguise and deception can be viewed as forms of ironic statement, since they work much the same as his double entendres: they invite us to share a secret and comic knowledge of Richard's true intention, which he wraps in the appearance of its very opposite. He assures us privately that he will capture the heart of the Lady Anne, whose father-in-law and husband he has recently slain, and then proceeds to amaze us by doing just that. He similarly undertakes to prove that the London populace can be prevailed upon to regard him as a pious recluse, studying divinity at all hours of the day and night and accepting only with the greatest reluctance the burdens of state thrust upon him by his importunate subjects—that is, by Buckingham and Catesby, who are also in on the joke. Throughout much of the play, Richard's plan seems to be succeeding. His view of human nature is an unattractive one, but it seems to be verifiable and so Richard is apparently justified in his ironic conclusions about human weakness. Every victim is blind to his own fate like Hastings, or prone to flattery like Anne, or ambitious like the Queen's kindred, or heir to the sins of his parents like young Prince Edward and his brother. Richard's ironic viewpoint is based on the grim comedy of man as his own worst enemy.

Yet Richard does not perceive, nor do we perceive at first, that he is preparing his own downfall just as the devil does in the N Town Passion play. Richard is part of a larger scheme of which he is ignorant until too late. An overseeing force, wishing to punish the English people for their crimes of mutual hatred and treachery, has raised up in their midst a genius of discord who will precipitate a frenzy of slaughter and then fall himself after having punished those who deserve to be punished. Richard's career thus exemplifies the "internal fatality" described by Kenneth Burke in his remarks on irony as prophecy: what rises will fall, and the very cause of the rise will contribute with ironic appropriateness and "inevitability" to the nature of the fall.[15] The ultimate joke is on Richard, and this last benign irony is one which the audience can wholeheartedly share—as it could not share in the sinister ironies of Richard's double entendres.

Irony as a criticism of life, then, leads alternatively to dispiriting or benign conclusions. The perception that men are foolish, self-blinded, and led by their own willfulness to destinies they have striven to avoid is often a pessimistic observation, even bitter (as, for example, in Aldous Huxley's *Point Counter Point*), but it need not be. Especially in medieval Christendom, the vanity of human wishes and the ironies attendant on such a view were usually regarded as part of a divine perspective. The famous conclusion of Chaucer's *Troilus and Cressida* is a case in point. Once Troilus has left the arena of his frustrated hopes and is able to look down on the smallness of his previous existence, what else should he do but laugh? Even today the notion of human folly as endearing and even protective is a frequent source of consolation. I read in a recent study of American attitudes on marriage, for example,[16] that Americans in overwhelming percentages rate themselves as very happily married and yet are gloomy about prospects for happiness in the marriages of their friends and neighbors. Well may we say with Antony, in *Antony and Cleopatra*, that "the wise gods seel our eyes."

Shakespeare makes use, in his tragedies, of two basic approaches to ironic structure. One approach, including all of the Roman or classical plays with the important exception of *Antony and Cleopatra*, looks upon the irony of man's fate as unredeemed by the benign vision that all is somehow ultimately for the best. Man's failure is noble because he struggles nobly and fortifies himself with resolution, but the consequences of action are ultimately futile and therefore dispiriting. In the non-Roman plays, on the other hand, a mysterious counterforce exerts itself so that evil is

15. Kenneth Burke, *A Grammar of Motives* (Berkeley and Los Angeles: University of California Press, 1969), app. D, "The Four Master Tropes."

16. *Life*, 17 November 1972, pp. 59–61.

to a greater or lesser extent foiled by its own machinations. These plays make use, to varying degrees, of the benignly ironic strategy employed in *Richard III*. This is not to say that the benign force at work is necessarily divine (*King Lear* is obviously problematic in this regard) or that the overall effect of these plays is ironic. Clearly *Othello* and *Lear* are not what we call ironic plays, despite their indebtedness to ironic method; we are more apt to apply the all-embracing label "ironic" to *Julius Caesar* and *Coriolanus*.

Let me outline the ironic pattern of the Roman plays with a brief look at *Julius Caesar*. The essential irony of *Julius Caesar* is that the noblest Roman of them all, Brutus, cannot command a noble revolution. The end he pursues, the restoration of the liberties of Rome, is not enhanced but diminished by everything he does. In part this is because Brutus does not understand the harsh exigencies of a *coup d'état*, and in part it is because Brutus does not fully know himself. However much he attempts to explain his own motives to himself, Brutus remains blind to the ironical resemblances between himself and the man he would supplant. We find of course ironies in Caesar's own character, as for instance when Caesar's vaunting assertions that he is above human weakness are juxtaposed with proofs of his deafness and superstition.[17] The irony of Brutus' character is that he is no less free of contradiction. Although there are differences as well, Brutus is like Caesar in being fixed in his opinion and unwilling to compromise. He refuses, for example, to consider the urgings of his fellow-conspirators to do away with Mark Antony and insists on allowing Antony to speak in Caesar's funeral. Most ironically of all, Brutus is like Caesar in being proud and prone to flattery. He is in part won over to the conspirators by Cassius' repeated comparing of his name with that of Caesar. "Brutus and Caesar: what should be in that 'Caesar'? / Why should that name be sounded more than yours?" (I, ii, 142–43). Brutus indeed has a notion of himself as the savior of Rome, the inheritor of a republican tradition begun by Lucius Junius Brutus. He

17. William Elton, *King Lear and the Gods* (San Marino, Calif.: Henry E. Huntington Library, 1966), p. 330.

sees himself as the man who must defy tyranny as his ancestors did before him.

Yet who is to succeed Caesar? The Roman citizens respond to Brutus' public oration, following the assassination, with the cry, "Let him be Caesar!" and "Caesar's better parts / Shall be crown'd in Brutus" (III, ii, 51–52). Brutus is of course too honorable to desire the crown he had denied Caesar. Still, he fails to perceive that the power vacuum created by Caesar's death will be filled by those who are unscrupulous in the use of power. Since Brutus is unwilling and unsuited to be the man on horseback demanded by the situation, Mark Antony and especially Octavius Caesar press relentlessly forward to seize the opportunity. The "tide in the affairs of men" cited earlier by Cassius as argument for swift action by the conspirators now mocks the leader of those conspirators who cannot or will not exercise the ruthless power sought so avidly by Antony and Octavius. Antony and Octavius calmly sign death warrants for their own kinsmen when necessary and cancel the bequests to the citizenry promised by Mark Antony in his public reading of Caesar's will. Meantime the revolutionary allies fall into disarray because Brutus cannot bring together the means and ends of revolution. The man who earlier had wished somehow to end Caesar's life without spilling his blood now cannot bring himself to support his financially troubled army by foraging on the land. Brutus and Cassius fall out over what appears to be a routine case of corruption in the army. Brutus' very nobility prevents him from making use of the opportunity to which his ideals have led him. The greatest victim of this ironic dilemma is Rome's republican tradition. Brutus the republican has helped set in motion one of the greatest periods of one-man rule in the history of civilization.

This ironic conclusion does not offer a sense that self-blinded men are led despite themselves to achievements that are for the best—unless, of course, one wants to argue that Roman imperialism is manifestly a benign result, a view for which the text gives no support. Accordingly, the play's fifth act presents us with an overwhelming series of ironic situations and statements that simply continue the im-

pression of noble and well-meant futility rather than alle-
viating it. For example, in the battle of Philippi, Brutus sets
too eagerly on Octavius and then is routed because his soldiers fall to spoil. Brutus the man of absolute integrity is
undone at the last by the sort of petty corruption and worldly
self-serving that he hates most, and by his own soldiers
(V,iii,7–8). In the same scene, Cassius commits suicide
when he thinks his dear friend Titinius has been captured;
ironically, in fact, things are going well for the conspirators
at this moment in the battle. Titinius arrives moments too
late to report the good news that Octavius has been thrown
back by Brutus' power. Messala's comment on Cassius' untimely suicide underscores the pattern whereby men leap to
their own confusion through misinterpretation of the circumstances that concern them most:

> O hateful error, melancholy's child,
> Why dost thou show to the apt thoughts of men
> The things that are not? O error, soon conceiv'd,
> Thou never com'st unto a happy birth, *(V, iii,*
> But kill'st the mother that engend'red thee! *67–71)*

Cassius himself has commented, just before his suicide, on
the irony that he is about to die on his birthday, an irony that
points to the larger sense in which so many men travel frantically through life in quest of a goal which they never
achieve, having to settle instead for fulfilling what was fore-
ordained. "Time is come round," says Cassius, "And where
I did begin, there shall I end" (V, iii, 23–24). Or, as Brutus
reflects a short time earlier, "O that a man might know /
The end of this day's business ere it come! / But it sufficeth
that the day will end, / And then the end is known" (V, i,
123–25).

Many are the expressions of a similarly ironic perception
in other Roman or classical plays. Troilus cries, "How my
achievements mock me!" when he learns that he must make
the personal decision to return Cressida to the Greeks in
order to allow Helen to continue living with Paris. Since
Troilus has earlier insisted, in the Trojan council of war, that
Helen is to be kept at all cost, he cannot now honorably
refuse to acquiesce to something that will deliver Antenor

from captivity. Coriolanus wryly observes, after he has ca-
pitulated to his mother for the last time and has agreed to
spare the city of Rome (which he so abhors) and by so doing
place his life in jeopardy, "The gods look down, and this
unnatural scene / They laugh at" (V, iii, 184–85). The history plays sometimes yield similar statements, as when
Prince Hal, weary of his companionship with Poins and his
tarnished reputation, observes, "Thus we play the fools with
the time, / and the spirits of the wise sit in the clouds and
mock us" (*II Henry IV*, II, ii, 134–35).

I should like to turn, however, to tragedies making use of
a pattern like that found in *Richard III*, one in which evil is
to a greater or lesser extent foiled by its own contrivances.
Romeo and Juliet, Shakespeare's earliest non-Roman tragedy,
invokes a benign counterforce that works ultimately to
man's advantage even though the benefit can be perceived
only in retrospect. "A greater power than we can contradict / Hath thwarted our intents," observes Friar Laurence
at the tomb, and Prince Escalus gives an even more expli-
citly benign interpretation of that "greater power" through
the recurring figure of oxymoron: "See what a scourge is
laid upon your hate, / That heaven finds means to kill your
joys with love" (V,iii,153–54, 292–93). As one critic has
perceptively written, the greatest irony in *Romeo and Juliet*
resides not in "such obvious peripeties as the slowness of
the bumbling friar or the early arrival at the tomb, but in the
fact that the play carries at every moment the idea both of
love's perfection and love's death."[18]

Hamlet offers the most important example among the
major tragedies of the pattern of the "beguiler beguiled."
Laertes sees too late that he is a "woodcock to mine own
springe" (V,ii,309). Hamlet, speaking of Rosencrantz and
Guildenstern, observes that "'tis the sport to have the engi-
ner / Hoist with his own petar" (III,iv,213–214). Not without reason, Horatio characterizes the story we have witnessed as one of "accidental judgments, casual slaughters, /
Of deaths put on by cunning and forc'd cause, / And, in
this upshot, purposes mistook / Fall'n on the inventors'

18. States, *Irony and Drama*, p. 32.

heads" (V,ii,384–387). For most participants, the ironic series of events whereby they are undone by their own contrivances is a punitive result, alleviated only to the extent
that a good-natured person like Laertes can see the justice
of his punishment and so can ask forgiveness while there is
still time. For Hamlet, on the other hand, the ironic twists
of the ending are ultimately benign. The rash action that
earlier led to the slaying of Polonius and thus to Hamlet's
banishment becomes at long last his friend, since the death
of Polonius leads to the angry return to Denmark of Laertes,
to the conspiracy with Claudius, and hence to the final duel
in which Laertes and Claudius are justly punished for their
treachery. Through a series of circumstances that neither
Hamlet nor any man could possibly foresee, a mysterious
overseeing power arranges the seemingly chaotic events of
Hamlet's story into one of ultimate justice. Although he is
prompted by his father's ghost to seek revenge, Hamlet
ironically finds that revenge only when he surrenders himself to the will of a higher power and is ready for what will
happen. Ironically, the Hamlet who has longed for death as
a surcease from his awful burden finds death in the unexpected fulfillment of his father's command.

    The other "great" tragedies partake to a greater or lesser
extent of a comparable pattern, even though none is an
"ironic" play when viewed as an artistic whole. We are hor-
rified by the ironies of the recurrent phrase "honest Iago"
and by the spectacle of Desdemona's "overzeal of innocence," as Coleridge calls it—her compassionate pleading
for Michael Cassio through which she hastens her own destruction.[19] Iago, the villain, is the apostle of self-control:
as he explains to Roderigo, "Our bodies are our gardens, to
the which our / wills are gardeners" (I, iii, 323–24). Yet at
last villainy outreaches itself in the familiar configuration of
the beguiler beguiled. Even though Iago prevails on Othello
to destroy Desdemona's life, he cannot prevent her sacrifice
from restoring Othello to a faith in her transcendent good-

    19. For an analysis of irony in *Othello*, see Sedgwick, *Of Irony*, pp.
52–55, 87–114, and Kenneth Burke, *"Othello*: An Essay to Illustrate a
Method," *Perspectives by Incongruity*, ed. Stanley Edgar Hyman (Bloom-
ington: Indiana University Press, 1964).

ness. Othello has destroyed her and is thus a tragic protagonist, but he knows—even if too late—that she was good.

In a similar vein, Edmund's machinations in *King Lear*
can prevail upon the Earl of Gloucester to banish and dis-
inherit his loyal son Edgar, but Edmund cannot prevent the
ultimate revelation of the truth and reconciliation of father
and son. Even Cordelia's sacrifice, despite its suggestion of
a disordered or indifferent cosmos at the very end of the
play, affirms a restored faith in humanity's potential for
goodness. The appalling ironies of inverted meaning in
words like "justice," "folly," and "natural" have yielded to
the infinitely more compassionate ironies at the play's
end—the irony, for example, of Edmund's inability to save
the life of Cordelia after he has belatedly seen the need for
contrition. Even if, as W. R. Elton has argued, the sequen-
tial ironies of the play continually mock those characters
who ask for divine assistance, warmth and love are ultimately provided by human characters acting as though the
gods still care.[20] In *Macbeth*, the reversal of the irony and
the resulting catharsis come to us by way of prophecies uttered by the witches and otherwordly spirits. The fearful
half-truths, uttered by the powers of darkness "to betray 's
in deepest consequence," do claim Macbeth and Lady Macbeth irretrievably, but later serve as affirmations of a just
nemesis (in the marching of Birnam Wood to Dunsinane and
in the equivocations about Macduff's birth of no woman)
and of a secure royal dynasty for Scotland.

Antony and Cleopatra may represent a synthesis of
Shakespeare's use of irony in tragedy, since it is at once a
Roman play and yet one in which the final peripety brings
with it an ambiguous sense that human blindness has not
resulted only in tragic error and failure. The character
Menecrates well expresses the sense in which man's self-
destructive urges are often benignly thwarted. "We, ignorant of ourselves, / Beg often our own harms," says Menecrates, "which the wise pow'rs / Deny us for our good; so
find we profit / By losing of our prayers" (II,i,5–8). Me-

20. Elton, *King Lear and the Gods*, p. 332. Also Northrop Frye,
Anatomy of Criticism (Princeton: Princeton University Press, 1957),
p. 237.

necrates aptly anticipates the way in which Antony and
Cleopatra surely lose their prayers in this play while the
remorselessly canny Caesar wins all; and yet to what end?
At the last, Caesar is the beguiler beguiled while Antony
and Cleopatra pursue a vision of mythic greatness. Even if
Antony is tricked by Cleopatra's wiles into undertaking a
comically inept suicide, even if we wonder whether Cleopatra is angling to the very end to entrap Caesar as one last
victim of her Circean charms, Antony still emerges as the
mythic Colossus or Hercules whose "legs bestrid the ocean"
and whose reared arm "Crested the world" (V, ii, 82–83).
The fallen world in which Antony and Cleopatra have been
vanquished fades into the insignificance of "The little O, the
earth." Our last vision of Cleopatra is of her in regal attire,
triumphantly addressing the asp at her breast: "O, couldst
thou speak, / That I might hear thee call great Caesar ass /
Unpolicied!" (V, ii, 306–8).

In a similar vein, the saddening ironies of the fallen
world in the tragicomedies repeatedly dissolve into a vision
of cosmic laughter. Leontes' insanely vindictive pursuit of
his innocent wife Hermione can elicit only dismay from his
courtiers; the business must move them "To laughter, as I
take it," as Antigonus says, "If the good truth were known"
(*Winter's Tale*, II, i, 199–200). Yet the tragicomedies insist
on a mysterious higher world that can play pranks on man
for his own benefit, restoring him to happiness when he
least deserves or expects it. "Fortune brings in some boats
that are not steer'd," observes Pisanio in *Cymbeline* (IV, iii,
4–6), in a recurring nautical metaphor for a benign providence operating through fate or circumstance as in *Pericles*.
And Lucius in *Cymbeline* comforts Imogen with a sentiment
that expresses more clearly than most the origins of this benignly ironic pattern in the Christian story of the fortunate
fall of man. "Some falls," says Lucius, "are means the hap-
pier to arise" (IV, ii, 403).

2 *Julius Caesar* and *Coriolanus*: Shakespeare's Roman World of Words

ANNE BARTON

On the eve of Caesar's assassination, when the heavens rain down fire and Rome is filled with prodigies and portents, Casca encounters Cicero in the streets. Breathless and dismayed, Casca pours out a tale of marvels, abnormalities which, he believes, must prefigure some calamity to the state. Cicero, who remains icily calm, admits that

(I, iii, 33–35)

> Indeed, it is a strange-disposed time;
> But men may construe things after their fashion,
> Clean from the purpose of the things themselves.

For Elizabethans, this warning of how language may misrepresent fact, how words—whether involuntarily or on purpose—can falsify phenomenal experience, must have seemed especially striking on the lips of Cicero: acknowledged grand master of the art of persuasion, the greatest orator and rhetorician of the ancient world. Shakespeare's Cicero makes no attempt himself to interpret the terrors of the night. He rests content with the neutral observation that disturbed skies such as these are not to walk in, then leaves the stage. In the very next moment, Cassius enters and Casca finds himself confronting a man who proceeds at once to construe things "clean from the purpose of the things themselves" and, what is more, makes Casca believe him. By the end of the scene, Casca has not only accepted Cassius' very different view of the tempest as a reflection of the diseased and monstrous condition of Rome under Caesar's rule, he has agreed as a result to join the conspirators and end that rule through an act of violence. In doing so, he helps to bring about precisely that cataclysm, that condition of anarchy and upheaval that, initially, he feared.

Although Cicero has no part in the action of *Julius Caesar*, it seems to have been important to Shakespeare that the audience should, from time to time, be reminded of his presence and of the controversy associated with his name. In the second scene of act I, Cicero passes across the stage twice as a member of Caesar's entourage. Brutus as bystander remarks on the discontent in his eyes. Casca says that after Antony's abortive effort to crown Caesar, Cicero spoke in Greek and that those who understood him smiled and shook their heads. In act II, after the scene with Casca, Cicero's name is introduced again when Brutus insists upon overruling his confederates and excluding him from the conspiracy on the highly suspect grounds that "he will never follow anything / That other men begin." At Sardis, in act IV, Cassius is shocked to learn that Cicero was one of the senators proscribed by the triumvirs and that he is dead. It is a scattered collection of references but, I believe, purposeful. By keeping the enormous memory of Cicero alive in his tragedy, Shakespeare constantly directs his audience's attention towards Rome as the city of orators and rhetoricians: a place where the art of persuasion was cultivated, for better or for worse, to an extent unparalleled in any other society.

The argument over the ethical status of oratory begins long before the time of Cicero. In the *Gorgias*, Plato allowed Socrates to tear the rhetoricians to shreds, on the grounds that their art creates spurious belief without instructing either the listeners or the practitioner in the nature of the Good. It is really a way of managing ignorant mankind through flattery and so not an art at all, properly considered, but an equivocal skill existing in the same relationship to the soul that elaborate cookery does to the body: the rhetorician makes things taste so nice that we swallow them whole, without inquiring into the true nature of the ingredients. Aristotle tried to rescue rhetoric from Plato's scorn. He made his own verdict that it was a genuine art quite plain by writing a treatise on the subject himself and by insisting

upon its close relationship with the truth-finding science of
Logic. Aristotle's *Rhetoric*, although it was to exert a powerful influence on Renaissance theories of style, nonetheless
managed to provide the enemy with valuable ammunition
by admitting that the justification of the orator's art lies in
the fact that an ignorant and uneducated public is incapable
of distinguishing truth from falsehood through the exercise
of reason and therefore needs to be persuaded through an
appeal to faculties other than the rational. This, of course,
is all very well provided that the orator himself can tell good
from evil, *and* happens to be an honest man. But what if he
is not? Montaigne, whose contempt for the arts of persuasion was positively withering, made use of Aristotle in his
own assault upon the rhetoricians. Oratory, he asserted, in
his essay "On the Vanitie of Words," is a cozening and de-
ceitful art devised "to busie, to manage, and to agitate a
vulgar and disordered multitude." In states where

the vulgar, the ignorant, or the generalities have had all the power,
as that of Rhodes, those of Athens and that of Rome, and where
things have ever beene in continuall disturbance and uproare,
thither have Orators and professors of that Art flocked.

The crucial position of Cicero in this venerable argument
is the result not only of his colossal reputation as the great
orator/statesman of antiquity and the creator of a model
prose style: it derives from his attempt to demonstrate, both
in his writing and in his own politicial career, that Plato's
gulf between rhetoric and philosophy could be closed—that
the great orator must also be a virtuous man and his art
dedicated to the service of truth and right action. On the
whole, Cicero emerges well from the scrutiny of Plutarch.
He seems to have been physically timid; he was childishly
vain of his own abilities and achievements and given to the
kind of personal sarcasm that makes needless enemies, but
his essential probity and his concern for the welfare and
continuance of the Roman republic are never in doubt. Yet,
even with Cicero, it is clear that precept and practice were
not always in accord. Plutarch records that he once turned
on a former client with the taunt: "Do you suppose you were
acquitted for your own merits, Munatius, and was it not that

I so darkened the case, that the court could not see your guilt?" For all his protestations to the contrary, Cicero was not above exercising his eloquence for its own sake, in defense of what he knew to be a bad cause. The anti-Ciceronian movement of the Renaissance was essentially stylistic in its concerns, but at least some of its adherents (notably Montaigne) reacted against Cicero's ornate prose precisely because those long, periodic sentences, with their hypnotic rhythms and massed, parallel clauses, seemed to them glib and insincere, an elevation of manner over matter in which truth was neglected or submerged.

Shakespeare's friend Ben Jonson was a notable anti-Ciceronian, a man who modeled his own prose on the curt and deliberately inharmonious style of Tacitus and Seneca. Despite this aesthetic predilection, he wrote a tragedy in which Cicero appears not as the background figure that he was in Shakespeare's *Julius Caesar* but as the hero. Jonson's *Catiline* (1611) also examines the Roman world of words, but it conducts this examination in a narrow and specialized way. The real gloss on *Catiline* is provided by Francis Bacon's little book, *Of the Colours of Good and Evil* (1597), a treatise designed to instruct readers in the difference between honest and dishonest rhetorical argument. Bacon, himself (of course) a distinguished orator, believed as strongly as Cicero that rhetoric, the science of moving the will, ought to be tied to the service of truth. As a political realist he was aware, however, that all too often it was not. Hence his desire to expose the tricks of the trade, to demonstrate how things in themselves good or evil may be colored by the skillful orator until they look like their opposites.

Jonson's *Catiline* is a kind of dramatic version of Bacon's *Colours of Good and Evil*. The action of the play, if you can call it that, consists almost entirely of a comparison of Cicero's style of persuasion with that of the villainous Catiline. Jonson's Cicero is no angel. He makes use of informers, administers bribes, doesn't always tell the truth, and occasionally acts outside the law. The political game in Rome enforces compromise of this kind. He is able, nonetheless, to save the republic: not only because he is intelligent, dedicated, and essentially honest, but because he can give these particular personal qualities a persuasive, linguistic shape. Although Cicero is what his enemies like to call an upstart consul, a new man not of senatorial rank, he makes words take the place of wealth, family, and influential connections. Catiline, superficially, is an effective speaker too. But Jonson is determined to show that for the intelligent auditor, the listener who also thinks, all of Catiline's arguments simply give him away for the man he is: false, violent, greedy, hysterical, and entirely destructive. To move from Catiline's speeches to those of Cicero is to exchange false rhetoric for true in a sense that Bacon and (for that matter) the historical Cicero would have understood.

The Elizabethans did not applaud Jonson's *Catiline*. Like its predecessor *Sejanus* (1603), Jonson's second Roman tragedy failed on the stage. It is difficult, for all the wit and intelligence of the play, not to sympathize with this original verdict. *Catiline* explores an issue as important in modern as in ancient political life, but it is curiously academic and circumscribed. Encumbered by Jonson's learning, and by a certain inflexibility and didacticism in its handling of the past, it is so much drama *à thèse* that it almost ceases to be drama at all. Jonson's original audience apparently liked the first two acts, tolerated the third, and broke into open revolt when asked to attend to Cicero's culminating oration—all three-hundred-odd lines of it—in act IV. It is tempting to believe that Shakespeare was at least partly to blame. After all, by 1611 London audiences had already seen *Julius Caesar* and *Coriolanus*: two tragedies which also focus on persuasion, on the pleasures and perils of rhetoric in ancient Rome, but which do so in a fashion not only far more dramatic than Jonson's but more wide-ranging, provocative and profound.

Both *Julius Caesar* and *Coriolanus* open with a scene of persuasion: "Before we proceed any further, hear me speak." The First Citizen in *Coriolanus* imposes a stay upon the violence of his rebellious companions purely in order to confirm them in it, to extract a concrete statement of hatred for Caius Marcius, and to give their purpose a linguistic shape. "Let us kill him, and we'll have corn at our price. Is't a verdict?" And the mob replies, "No more talking on't; let it be done." But the Second Citizien is not so sure. "One word," he begs, "good citizens." The scene resolves itself into a debate between two speakers, one radical, the other moderate, with the crowd poised irresolutely in between. The arrival of the patrician Menenius merely extends this debate.

> What work's, my countrymen, in hand?
> Where go you
> With bats and clubs? The matter? Speak, I pray you.

Menenius, of course, has come to persuade. His tale of the belly, a tale told in figurative, deliberately beguiling verse, is intended to sway the citizens and reduce them to patience. They themselves know this. "Well, I'll hear it, sir: yet you must not think to fob off our disgrace with a tale," the First Citizen tells him defensively, in his characteristic prose. Menenius begins his story. Halfway through, something startling happens. The radical First Citizen becomes entangled in the fiction. Not only does he begin to act out one of the parts implied, he abandons his own prose idiom for the blank verse of the patrician.

> The kingly-crowned head, the vigilant eye,
> The counsellor heart, the arm our soldier,
> The steed the leg, the tongue our trumpeter,
> With other muniments and petty helps
> In this our fabric.

Even Menenius is astonished by this sudden alteration in the citizen's style: "'Fore me, this fellow speaks! What then? what then?"

Although the First Citizen is still arguing his own case against the lords of Rome, accusing the belly in the name of the discontented other members of the body, he has accepted the rhetorical framework of the argument proposed by the patrician. The way now lies open for him to be convinced by that apparently logical conclusion towards which Menenius' story is heading: a story whose terms he has granted

and in which he has allowed himself to become an actor.
When the patrician presents the belly's self-vindication, the
First Citizen grudgingly accepts it: "It was an answer," he
admits. "How apply you this?" Menenius is more than halfway to victory, a victory achieved solely through the power
of words. The citizens of Rome are no better off materially
at the end of his story than they were at the beginning, no
less ragged or hungry, but the situation no longer seems
clear-cut. None of them notice that Menenius' argument is
really a false "colour" in Bacon's sense, that it craftily
avoids the question of what to do when the belly, as is the
case in Rome, refuses to fulfill its function of distributing
food to the other members of the body politic. They have
been dazzled by words. "Nay, these are almost thoroughly
persuaded," Menenius says a few moments later. And, indeed, they have ceased to be a convinced and dangerous mob.

At just this point, Caius Marcius makes his first appearance in the play. He proceeds at once to tell the citizens
what, for him, they are—scabs and curs, hares and geese—
and to undermine Menenius' accomplished oratory by at-
tacking its very basis: "He that will give good words to thee
will flatter / Beneath abhorring." The accusation itself
reaches back to Plato's *Gorgias*, to the immemorial distrust
of the rhetorician as a man who feeds soothing lies to the
people, whose skill is that of a flatterer. With Coriolanus,
however, this ancient distrust has assumed a new and individual psychological form. I think myself that Shakespeare
meant us to see Volumnia's son as a kind of anachronism in
the Rome of this play: the lonely survivor of a vanished and
more primitive past. When Cominius, in act II, proposes
Coriolanus for consul before the assembled senators, he
chooses his words carefully.

> It is held
> That valour is the chiefest virtue, and
> Most dignifies the haver: if it be,
> The man I speak of cannot in the world
> Be singly counterpoised.

There is no equivalent to those hesitant phrases, "It is held" and "if it be," in Shakespeare's source. Plutarch had stated simply that "in those days valiantness was honoured in Rome above all other virtues; which they call *virtus*, by the name of virtue itself, as including in that general name all other special virtues besides." The hint of doubt is Shakespeare's invention. Cominius seems, as a result, to speak out of some uneasy awareness that Roman society is in a state of transition, that around him traditional priorities are being modified, or even displaced. Although he loves and admires the epic warrior Coriolanus, Cominius can see that a new and more complicated Rome is gradually replacing the old: one in which the plebeians must have a voice as well as the patricians, in which peace will be a condition more highly prized than war, and words quite as important as heroic deeds. Cominius is not the only patrician to accept, without necessarily liking, this change—which is why Coriolanus, later on, will be able to see himself as betrayed by the members of his own class.

On three separate occasions in the tragedy, Coriolanus is identified with a dragon. The word stands out sharply from its surrounding verbal context. Enormous, impressive, but somehow obsolete, the protagonist of this play is indeed a kind of fabulous beast. A dragon may, under certain special circumstances, be a very useful thing for a city to possess. In time of war, you open the gates and let it loose, and it proceeds to strike the enemy like a planet, annihilating the opposition. The trouble comes later, when peace has been restored and the dragon—its occupation gone—is left to lumber about the marketplace in full armor, upsetting the vegetable stalls and breathing fire on the tradesmen. It is now an embarrassment more than an assset. There is a sense in which the gods have been unkind to Coriolanus by creating him, at this particular moment of historical time, as a Roman and not a Volscian. Volscian society, as we see it in the play, exists at a much more primitive stage of development. Loose-knit, scattered, and essentially feudal rather than civic, it seems to be based upon personal loyalties and professionally dedicated to war. There is no apparent division of interest between the upper and lower classes. Even the servingmen at Aufidius' house in Antium are overjoyed to hear that they are to have "a stirring world again," where their Roman equivalents had been dismayed. For these Volscian plebeians, war exceeds peace "as far as day does night." Indeed, they recognize that war holds their entire society together. In peace, men "less need one another" and so are likely to quarrel among themselves. Apart from Aufidius, who is eaten up with jealousy of Coriolanus, the Volscians are unanimous in their opinion as to what you do when you suddenly acquire a dragon: you fall down and worship it. Then, you make sure to keep it employed. "He is their god," Cominius says ruefully, and Aufidius' lieutenant tells his master that the Volscian soldiers use Coriolanus "as the grace 'fore meat, / Their talk at table and their thanks at end." It was never so in Rome.

Whatever their other virtues, dragons are rarely social animals. Neither is Coriolanus, and this fact is reflected in the way he uses language. In a city where everyone, with the significant exception of Coriolanus' wife Virgilia, is a kind of rhetorician—even the citizens, you remember, in the first scene, were unable to fire the Capitol without stopping to hold a debate on the way—Coriolanus stands out as a man who fears and despises words. I do not mean by this that he is inarticulate, a "languageless land fish," as Thersites calls Ajax in *Troilus and Cressida*. Coriolanus can be most eloquent on occasion, but it is an eloquence of a curious and self-defeating kind.

Language is preeminently an instrument of communication. The art of rhetoric is the art of moving the wills of other human beings, persuading them to adopt a course of action that the orator believes—or pretends to believe—is right. Coriolanus' eloquence is not like this, and not all the efforts of his mother and friends can effect a transformation before it is too late. Whether he is reviling the mob in the first scene of the play, and so undoing the careful oratory of Menenius, or haranguing the patricians in act III in terms that embarrass them far more than the tribunes, this man speaks in a vacuum. He says what he feels, unpacks his heart with words, without deigning to consider the effect on the audience or the requirements of the occasion. So, in

act I, he tries to rally exhausted soldiers with an oration of
which Caliban might have been proud:

> All the contagion of the south light on you,
> You shames of Rome! You herd of—Boils and plagues
> Plaster you o'er, that you may be abhorr'd
> Further than seen and one infect another
> Against the wind a mile!

When, after completing this exhortation, Coriolanus rushes
through the gates of Corioli, not a man goes with him. And
one sees why. The Roman soldiers later make a sword of
him, and so win the city, but not because of anything he
says. The Coriolanus who reappears, miraculously alive,
from the enemy town he entered alone is an object visually
so horrific—Cominius thinks at first that he is looking at
someone who has been flayed and is still walking—that the
troops are shocked, for a little while, into committing themselves wholly to this bloodstained emblem of War.

Even as Jonson was to do in *Catiline* a few years later,
Shakespeare constantly measures the public utterances of
Coriolanus against those of more effective speakers: Menenius, Cominius, even Volumnia and the tribunes. The result,
however, is not so much an investigation of the colors of
good and evil as it is of the impossibility of a man trying to
live in any society—let alone that of Rome—while repu-
diating and refusing to come to terms with the power of
words. Nothing in this tragedy has aroused more critical
disagreement than the question of Coriolanus' passionate
dislike of the praises of his friends. Is it sincere and becoming modesty that he displays after Corioli, when he repels
the "acclamations hyperbolical" of Cominius and the army,
when he flings out of the Senate rather than listen to an
account of his own heroic deeds? Or does the attitude spring
from arrogance, the vanity of a lonely man who rejects the
approval of the community because he wants to reserve his
exploits for himself, refusing to share them with anyone
else? I think myself that both of these interpretations are
wide of the mark. When Coriolanus claims that "I had
rather have my wounds to heal again / Than hear say how

I got them," or admits that "oft / When blows have made me stay, I fled from words," he seems to be gesturing towards some deep-rooted fear of language that he himself only half understands.

We must use words to interpret and also to perpetuate and remember phenomenal experience. Yet a thing described, whether it is a battle or the nature of an individual, can never be quite the same as the thing itself. Sometimes, the use of language to express fact results in gross distortion, in a picture of things that is "clean from the purpose of the things themselves," as Cicero warned. At other times, the falsification is only slight: the necessary concomitant of translation onto another level. It is inevitable, however, that facts should in some measure be transformed by being spoken about—and it is precisely this transformation that Coriolanus cannot endure. A man who "rewards his deeds with doing them," as Cominius says, whose proper sphere is that of action, of a sword arm "timed with dying cries," he resists the idea that words should be able to violate the integrity of events. Language contaminates the purity of action. It complicates things that initially were simple, overlays heroic certainties with qualifications which arise outside the moment of time as it was physically experienced. To admit alien factors of this kind, even when they seem most propitious to his own image, as they do in the praises of friends, is for Coriolanus to "monster" deeds, to soil action through words, and he feels especially vulnerable. After all, what is the point of being a dragon, an epic hero on the plains of Troy, if the entire achievement can be wiped out by a scrawny little official who says, "Traitor," or by the simple word, "Boy"? Cominius means well when he says, "If I should tell thee o'er this thy day's work / Thou't not believe thy deeds." For the man he is praising, however, that statement holds another and sinister kind of truth.

It is not Coriolanus' idea to stand for consul but that of his mother and friends. He himself would rather serve the Roman people "in my way / Than sway with them in theirs." He is right, but he allows himself to be persuaded to enter an alien world. By ancient law, Coriolanus must "speak to the people" before his office can be confirmed. He must display his wounds in the marketplace and consent himself to violate his own heroic past by describing it. From this point on, the people of Rome are referred to almost obsessively as "voices." "Sir," says Sicinius, "the people must have their voices." The word carries the simple meaning of an oral vote, but it also and more significantly suggests disembodied sound: language incarnate. There are forty-eight occurrences of the word *voice* or *voices* in *Coriolanus*, virtually all of them in this connection, far outstripping the incidence of the term in any other play. "If he do require our voices, we ought not to deny him . . . if he show us his wounds and tell us his deeds, we are to put our tongues into those wounds and speak for them." In *Julius Caesar*, Mark Antony too had talked of putting "a tongue / In every wound of Caesar that should move / The stones of Rome to rise and mutiny." But Caesar's flesh was insensible and dead: that of Coriolanus is irritably alive and wincing. Between his battle scars and the human tongue there is an invincible enmity. As he pointed out after Corioli, "I have some wounds upon me, and they smart / To hear themselves remembered." The image of citizens, men who do not themselves wield swords, mere opinion personified, intruding their tongues into the scars and cicatrices of honor, becomes, in this context, oddly strained and unpleasant.

Predictably, Coriolanus fails to see that the people who file past him "by ones, by twos and by threes" as he stands in the Forum are, for the moment at least, individuals and not a mob. After the battle of Corioli, he could not remember the name of the poor man, now a prisoner, who once befriended him in the city. Now, he is unable to see the people whose support he needs as anything but voices: noises that degrade his clean, lonely world of action. The price of the consulship, as the First Citizen points out, is "to ask it kindly"—not only gently, but in a fashion that admits a shared humanity. This the dragon cannot do. Later, on the way to the Senate in act III, Coriolanus' rage at discovering that Hydra has changed its collective mind and disallowed his election concentrates oddly on the tribune's word "shall": "It is a mind / That shall remain a poison where it is; / Not poison any further." Coriolanus returns in increasing fury to what he calls this "absolute shall" no fewer than five times, as though the word itself, a simple verb which Sicinius is making equivalent to an action, were the real enemy. The tribunes are not fools. Noting the astonishing effect of "shall," they decide the next time around to try the far more emotive word *traitor*, and the day is won.

Up to a point, Volumnia shares her son's attitude to words. "Hadst thou foxship," she says contemptuously to the tribunes in act IV, "to banish him that struck more blows for Rome / Than thou hast spoken words?" She possesses, nonetheless, a healthy respect for the art of oratory.

> Now it lies you on to speak
> To th' people, not by your own instruction,
> Nor by the matter which your heart prompts you,
> But with such words that are but roted in
> Your tongue, though but bastards and syllables
> Of no allowance to your bosom's truth.

In the second scene of act III, she not only scripts a speech for Coriolanus, but instructs him how to act it out with appropriate stage gestures: hat outstretched in hand, one knee kissing the ground in mock humility. "For in such business / Action is eloquence." Volumnia is tragically unable to see how such a phrase, and the equal weighting of doing and saying that lies behind it, attacks Coriolanus where he is most insecure. The arts of the orator and the actor are, of course, closely akin, the one shading into the other. The actor is a man whose profession requires him to speak words at secondhand, syllables learned by rote, which create a fictional situation. Coriolanus, for whom the whole idea of the theater is abhorrent, struggles hard to decline the "part" which his mother and Cominius are urging him to discharge. "Come, come, we'll prompt you," they promise, but Coriolanus fears that the performance he is being asked to put on may somehow contaminate his soul.

> I will not do't;
> Lest I surcease to honor mine own truth,
> And by my body's action teach my mind
> A most inherent baseness.

Plato, who distrusted the actors as much as he did the rhetoricians, would have sympathized. Men should not, he declared in the *Republic*, "depict or be skilful at imitating any
kind of illiberality or baseness, lest from imitation they
come to be what they imitate."

Paradoxically, although Coriolanus scarcely tries in the
Forum to follow the advice of his friends, once he has been
banished he becomes both an orator and an actor. There is
something oddly "staged" about his dignified farewell to
Volumnia, Virgilia, and the nobles at the beginning of act
IV, as though he were consciously playing a stoic's part
without believing in it. Of the two promises that he makes
in this scene—

> While I remain above the ground, you shall
> Hear from me still, and never of me aught
> But what is like me formerly—

both are immediately broken. At the end of the act, Menenius is admitting that no one has heard anything from Coriolanus in exile, not even his wife and mother. The first news,
moreover, that they receive of him—that he has joined with
Aufidius—is so opposite to everything that was like him
formerly that Menenius refuses at first to believe it. Shakespeare's stage direction in the First Folio, "Enter Coriolanus
in mean apparel, disguis'd and muffled," makes it quite
clear that the man who, in the Roman Forum, wore the traditional gown of humility with loathing, in a spirit that con-
tradicted its meaning, chooses to appear at Antium in rags.
And he proceeds, for the first time in his life, to use language to get something from an enemy. Aufidius is persuaded by Coriolanus' rhetoric: "O Martius, Martius! /
Each word thou hast spoke hath weeded from my heart / A
root of ancient envy." Only one act earlier, the ancient envy
of the citizens of Rome had been precisely the quality Coriolanus refused to try to uproot through the arts of oratory
and disguise. It is not merely Rome that Coriolanus betrays
here in act IV. He also betrays himself.

In most of the scenes in which she appears, Coriolanus'
wife Virgilia is an almost voiceless presence. He himself

calls her "my gracious silence." Volumnia and Valeria, those two eminently articulate ladies, occasionally torment her into speech, but she does not talk readily or of her own accord. She is also, as it seems, proof against persuasion. When her mother-in-law and Valeria try to get her to leave the house in act I and visit "the good lady that lies in," Virgilia makes no attempt to argue with them. Like Sir Thomas Browne, presumably, she knows that one may be "in as just a possession of Truth as of a City, and yet be forced to surrender" by entering a dispute. Virgilia advances no reasons for remaining at home. She has simply determined to do so, and she does. For all her timidity and tears, Virgilia is like Coriolanus as no one else in the play, including Volumnia, is like him. This is why she makes so devastating a suppliant in act V and why she, of all the women, speaks first. There is a sense in which her simple greeting, "my lord and husband," made to a man who seconds before was talking about standing as author of himself and knowing no other kin, is more deadly than all the oratory of Menenius, Cominius, and even Volumnia. This is language made bare and irreducible, virtually inseparable from fact, the language in which Coriolanus himself once believed. Even before Volumnia begins to plead, Coriolanus' pretense is doomed, indeed has been from the moment he saw the women approaching: "Like a dull actor now / I have forgot my part, and I am out, / Even to a full disgrace." Humbly, he admits to being the thing he had repudiated so fiercely before: an actor. The performance, moreover, has not even the dignity of tragedy. "Behold, the heavens do ope, / The gods look down, and this unnatural scene / They laugh at."

Coriolanus himself never progresses much beyond this moment of insight in which he holds his mother by the hand, "silent," as the stage direction indicates, and endures in the stillness the derisory laughter of gods for whom such spectacles of suffering and human pain are merely comical. Aufidius, for one thing, prevents him from being able to do anything with his dearly bought self-knowledge. Shakespeare inverted his normal tragic pattern at the end of *Coriolanus*. He made the scene in which the women are brought with drums and trumpets into the city, in which order is restored to Rome, precede the death of Coriolanus at Corioli. On the whole, Shakespeare seems to have been far more optimistic than most of his contemporaries in his belief that men and women do have the power to transform themselves, to alter old habits, engrained personality traits, even after maturity. The comedies, above all, proclaim this faith. There is something touching about the little oration which Coriolanus makes to the Volscians, both nobles and plebeians, assembled in the marketplace of Corioli in the final scene: "I am returned your soldier." With Aufidius at Antium, he had simply snarled out what seemed to him to be the truth—and the outrageousness—of his personal predicament, made a proposal to an individual of his own class, and hoped for the best. Here, at Corioli, he seems at last to have accepted the idea that his actions require explanation to the community at large, and that this can be done only by himself, through the medium of language. Without lying to the citizens, he nonetheless tries to shape words in such a way that they will communicate with a crowd of people he knows he has wronged, and will make the Volscians understand that he still belongs to them and that they have really not lost very much by making this peace. He is using language like a social being, not like a dragon.

Aufidius, unfortunately, is shrewd enough to suspect that fundamentally Coriolanus has not changed, that the man who makes this speech still cherishes a deep fear and mistrust of words. He acts accordingly:

> at his nurse's tears
> He whin'd and roar'd away your victory,
> That pages blush'd at him, and men of heart
> Look'd wond'ring each at other. . . .
> Name not the god, thou boy of tears.

This malicious description of the most profound and important moment of Coriolanus' life, that in which he silently took Volumnia's hand and came to terms at last with his own humanity, represents an extreme distortion of fact by dishonest speech. It is far worse than the accusation "traitor," a word which by now is almost an old friend. The meeting with the women, outside Rome, was not like this. But how is anyone to know? Aufidius—who declared at the time that he himself was "moved withal"—has rendered the episode unrecognizable. Coriolanus can almost be excused for reacting in the insane way he does to a violation of truth so painful and demeaning. Goaded beyond endurance, he not only forgets everything he has learned at such cost: he commits a sin of which previously he had never been guilty. "Like an eagle in a dove-cote, I / Flutter'd your Volscians in Corioles. / Alone I did it." Bragging hysterically about his dragonhood of the past, Coriolanus goes to his death like an animal: torn and dismembered by the other members of the pack.

In the Rome of *Coriolanus*, rhetoric is often a highly dubious commodity. Menenius, Volumnia, the tribunes, and the Volscian Aufidius all use it upon occasion to falsify fact. Nevertheless, tricky and dangerous though they are, words are still the necessary tools with which a society is built and maintained. To reject the arts of persuasion out of hand, to minimize language, is to become either as passive and limited in one's activities as Virgilia or else a lonely dragon like Coriolanus himself. This is especially true in a society like the one presented in this play: a Rome which is in the process of developing new and more sophisticated values and political forms. These new ideas and structures are, to a large extent, the creation of language: the product of argument and discussion among human beings. Rhetoric, in this process, has an honest as well as a suspect part to play. It was only when he wrote about the later republic, about a city become stagnant, its democratic institutions corrupt and decayed, that Shakespeare treated Roman oratory as something unequivocally poisonous: the ruin both of individuals and of the state.

Although *Julius Caesar* was written eight or nine years before *Coriolanus*, the Rome it depicts is historically much later: a dying republic that has outlived its earlier vitality and is about to collapse into some kind of dictatorship, whether that of Caesar or Octavius. It is a city of professional persuaders. Brutus and Cassius are even unable to have a private quarrel without a lunatic poet, that neither of them has ever seen before, bursting into the tent unannounced to urge, grandiloquently, that they "Love and be friends, as two such men should be." This, in effect, is the kind of democracy about which Montaigne was so scathing, where things are in "continuall disturbance and uproare," and orators and teachers of that art take advantage of the power they have over a fickle and disordered multitude. Montaigne regarded this syndrome as a powerful argument in favor of monarchy.

> For, that foolishnesse and facilitie, which is found in the common multitude, and which doth subject the same, to be managed, perswaded, and led by the eares, by the sweet alluring and sense-entrancing sound of this harmonie, without duly weighing, knowing, or considering the trueth of things by the force of reason: This facultie and easie yeelding, I say, is not so easily found in one only ruler, and it is more easie to warrant him from the impression of this poyson, by good institution and sound counsell.

It is interesting to note, in the light of Montaigne's belief, that Shakespeare's Caesar sees his own greatness partly in terms of his unpersuadability. Constant as the northern star, "that unassailable holds on his rank, / Unshak'd of motion," his blood—or so he claims—cannot "be thaw'd from the true quality / With that which melteth fools—I mean sweet words." In point of fact, Caesar has not escaped the general malaise of his city. He is present, fatally, in the Senate to speak these words only because he has been persuaded by Decius Brutus that, looked at properly, Calphurnia's ominous dream is flattering and propitious. Not until the final section of the tragedy does the genuinely unpersuadable man make his appearance. Shakespeare waited on the whole until *Antony and Cleopatra* to examine the character traits of Octavius, but the outline is already clear in the earlier play.

> *Ant:* Octavius, lead your battle softly on
> Upon the left hand of the even field.

> *Oct:*   Upon the right hand I. Keep thou the left.
> *Ant:*   Why do you cross me in this exigent?
> *Oct:*   I do not cross you; but I will do so.

End of argument.

Julius Caesar, like *Coriolanus*, opens with a scene of persuasion. The Roman citizens in this play, however, are entirely passive: mere puppets manipulated by others. They do not engage in debate as their equivalents do in *Coriolanus*, neither among themselves nor with the tribune Flavius. The cobbler, the carpenter, and their associates arrive in holiday attire, intending to shout themselves hoarse at great Caesar's triumph. When Flavius has finished speaking to them, they vanish ("tongue-tied," as he says contemptuously) to their homes, obscurely certain without any reasons having been advanced that Caesar is a bad thing, while Pompey was somehow splendid. They will reverse themselves quite as irrationally in act II, with far more serious consequences, when Brutus makes the tactical mistake of permitting Mark Antony to speak last—the position which the historical Cicero always advocated—in Caesar's funeral.

Public oratory in *Julius Caesar* is slick and professional as it never is in *Coriolanus*. Flavius, unlike Menenius, has been reading textbooks in the art of rabble-rousing. With its carefully spaced rhetorical questions, deceptive logic, emotive vocabulary, and hypnotic repetitions—"And do you now put on your best attire? / And do you now cull out a holiday? / And do you now strew flowers"—his speech is calculated to drown reason in passion. So, of course, is Antony's even more accomplished appeal to the crowd later on. Nonetheless, although Antony immediately turns the mutiny he has stirred up to his own political advantage— even truncating those legacies to the people of which he had made such capital in describing Caesar's will—he does at least share some of the emotion that he arouses in others on behalf of Caesar dead. "That I did love thee, Caesar, O, 'tis true." Flavius' tears for Pompey, on the other hand, are purely crocodilian. His real reason for tampering with the citizens emerges only after they have slunk guiltily off the stage:

> These growing feathers pluck'd from Caesar's wing
> Will make him fly an ordinary pitch,
> Who else would soar above the view of men
> And keep us all in servile fearfulness.

This is the hidden but real issue, not only of Flavius' speech but of much of the play.

Almost all the talk about democracy, freedom, tyranny, and restraint in *Julius Caesar* is really a camouflage for something else. Shakespeare's Caesar happens to be deaf in one ear, childless, subject to epileptic fits, vain, superstitious, and as likely to drown in a wintry river or succumb to a fever as soon as any other mortal. Despite these obvious shortcomings, he is also a Colossus: a man over life-size who has created and can control an empire. Cassius says angrily that "this man / Is now become a god," but the real difficulty is that he has not. Gods, after all, are exempt from our envy precisely because they belong to a different order of being. Competition is out of the question, and so is the kind of jealousy that springs from a resented inferiority. Caesar's various human failings are really more exacerbating than his genius, because they remind lesser men, running in the same race with the same handicaps, that they have been far outstripped. Cassius articulates this response most fully, but it is one that many other Roman patricians share, not least—as Cassius knows—the noble Brutus.

In *Julius Caesar*, the art of persuasion has come to permeate life so completely that people find themselves using it not only to influence others but to deceive themselves. This is true, above all, of Brutus. Brutus is competent enough as a public orator, although he lacks the fire and subtlety of Mark Antony, but his real verbal ingenuity declares itself only when he is using the techniques of oratory to blind himself and (occasionally) his friends. In the orchard soliloquy of act II, Brutus extracts purpose and resolve not from the facts of the situation but from a collection of verbal nothings: from words like "may" and "would."

There is no tangible basis for Brutus' fears of Caesar. Indeed, as he admits, observation and circumstance suggest the contrary. He is driven, as a result, to do the thing for which he secretly longs—kill Caesar—purely on the basis of a grammatical construction: a verbal emptiness which pretends to have the status of a fact. "Then lest he may, prevent." Antony had said of Caesar earlier in the play that his words were precisely equivalent to deeds: "When Caesar says, 'Do this,' it is performed." Brutus too tries to blur the distinction between speech and action, but the effect he creates is one of self-delusion rather than power.

Shakespeare's Caesar likes to refer to himself in the third person. "Speak, Caesar is turned to hear," he says to the soothsayer in act I, and in later scenes he resorts to this kind of self-naming almost obsessively. Shakespeare knew, of course, that the historical Caesar had written his commentary on the Gallic Wars in the third person, but there is more behind the mannerism (with Caesar as with General de Gaulle in our own time) than a mere literary practice. Self-naming implies taking oneself very seriously. It is a deliberately grand way of regarding one's own identity, as though that identity were already matter for historians. Antony is never guilty of it in *Julius Caesar*. He delivers all of his great oration in the first person. Brutus, by contrast, not only employs this peculiarly Roman form of the royal "we" in his defense to the citizens, he uses the third person repeatedly in private conversation. "Brutus," he tells Cassius, "had rather be a villager / Than to repute himself a son of Rome / Under these hard conditions." The effect of these persistent presentations of Brutus by Brutus as a somehow externalized object is to suggest that, although this man is in many ways noble, he is also far too aware of the fact. Indeed, it suggests an underlying affinity with Caesar: the man Brutus kills, supposedly, because Caesar was ambitious.

Cassius plays upon this failing. His persuasion is as deadly as it is because it recognizes and takes advantage of a deeply buried jealousy of Caesar, lurking behind all of Brutus' avowed republican principles, a jealousy which happens to be less conscious than his own. He harps upon

Brutus as public figure, the cynosure of every eye, whose ancestors drove the kings from Rome: a man whose scope and potentialities for greatness have somehow been cabined, cribb'd, confin'd by the rival presence of Caesar. He makes Brutus feel that he must commit a spectacular public act in order to validate his name. In doing this, Cassius is less than honest. His victim, however, not only plays into his hands but betters his instruction.

In the orchard soliloquy of act II, Brutus turned the techniques of oratory against his own conscience. He continues to do this throughout the remainder of the play. The man who pretends, in act IV, that he does not know about his wife's death, purely in order to impress Messala with the superhuman fortitude of the hero encountering pain, also tries to delude himself that the conspiracy is a kind of holy league. This is why he refuses to countenance an oath to bind its members. Even worse, he uses language dishonestly (much as Othello does after him) when he tries to persuade the conspirators that Caesar's death will be not a butchery but a religious sacrifice:

> We all stand up against the spirit of Caesar,
> And in the spirit of men there is no blood.
> O, that we then could come by Caesar's spirit,
> And not dismember Caesar.

They must, he claims, be "called purgers, not murderers." The names make all the difference.

In the event, the spirit of Caesar is precisely the thing they do not kill. They merely release it from the shackles of its human form and failings. No longer deaf, arrogant, epileptic, or subject to error, this spirit walks abroad as a thing against which, now, there is no defense. At Philippi, it turns the swords of the conspirators into their own proper entrails. It raises up a successor in the form of Octavius, who will annihilate the republic in Rome. Even before this happens, Brutus' appeal to the transforming power of words has become half desperate. In the spirit of men there is no blood. But blood, in the first scene of act III, is the element in which the conspirators are drenched. It dyes all of them scarlet, sticks to hands as well as to daggers, disgustingly daubs their faces and their clothes. Not even Brutus can pretend not to notice the sheer physical mess. Characteristically, he tries to spiritualize it, to alter its character by linguistic means:

> Stoop, Romans, stoop,
> And let us bathe our hands in Caesar's blood
> Up to the elbows, and besmear our swords:
> Then walk we forth, even to the market-place,
> And waving our red weapons o'er our heads,
> Let's all cry, "Peace, freedom, and liberty!"

Blood is not blood, he insists, but purely symbolic. It stands for the idea of freedom. The euphemism, and the action with which it is connected, is one of which the second half of the twentieth century has heard all too much.

Like Coriolanus, Brutus ends almost where he began. Rome moves on, and leaves both men behind. The last words of Brutus are not furious, like those of Coriolanus, but they are equally hard to accept. "In all my life," he says proudly, "I found no man but he was true to me." In Shakespeare, although not in Plutarch, Messala has already defected to Caesar, as Strato bitterly points out. Nor will time to come necessarily endorse Brutus' last vision of himself: a vision in which, characteristically, he is still presenting himself in the third person.

> I shall have glory by this losing day
> More than Octavius and Mark Antony
> By this vile conquest shall attain unto.
> So fare you well at once; for Brutus' tongue
> Hath almost ended his life's history.

Dante, after all, placed Brutus beside Judas Iscariot in the seventh circle of Hell.

Antony, as one might expect, is generous. "This was the noblest Roman of them all." He leaves us with the image of a Brutus who was gentle, devoid of envy, and perfectly temperate and well balanced: not at all the Brutus who was vulnerable to the persuasions of Cassius, the rash and intemperate man of the quarrel in act IV, who gave the word too early at Philippi. "In your bad strokes, Brutus, you give

good words," Antony had said shrewdly before. He forgets
these criticisms now. Funeral orations tend, of course, to be
false—whether out of good will and compassion for the
dead, or because it seems necessary now to tidy everything
up in accordance with the demands of piety and decorum.
"Let's make the best of it," one of the Volscian lords urges
at the end of *Coriolanus*, after Aufidius and the crowd have
with some difficulty been made to stop trampling on the
body. Even Aufidius, the man who planned and executed
Coriolanus' murder in the coldest of cold blood, announces
penitently that his rage is gone, "and I am struck with sorrow." Here, especially, the rhetoric rings false. Antony's en-
comium on the dead Brutus comes nearer truth, but it is far
from satisfactory or complete. The meanings inherent in the
stories of Coriolanus and of Brutus cannot be extracted from
funeral orations. They require language of another kind:
language that is both further from the facts of the situation
and, in another sense, closer. Plato did not like the poets
any more than he did the actors and rhetoricians. Nevertheless, it is in Shakespeare's two Roman plays that the truth
about Brutus and Coriolanus now seems to live.

3 Two Scenes from *Macbeth*

HARRY LEVIN

Hamlet without the Prince would still be more of a spectacle than *Macbeth* without the Thane of Glamis. Though the latter is not introspective by nature, his soliloquizing is central to the play, as he considers intentions, casts suspicions, registers hallucinations, coerces his conscience, balances hope against fear, and gives thought to the unspeakable—all this while sustaining the most energetic role in the most intense of Shakespeare's plays. *Macbeth* is the fastest of them, as Coleridge pointed out, while *Hamlet*, at almost twice its length, is the slowest. Thus the uncut *Hamlet* has plenty of room for other well-defined characters and for highly elaborated subplots. Whereas *Macbeth*, which has come down to us in a version stripped for action, concentrates more heavily upon the protagonist. He speaks over thirty per cent of the lines; an overwhelming proportion of the rest bear reference to him; and Lady Macbeth has about eleven per cent, all of them referring to him directly or indirectly. Most of the other parts get flattened in this process, so that his may stand out in bold relief. Otherwise, as Dr. Johnson commented, there is "no nice discrimination of character." As Macbeth successively murders Duncan, Banquo, and Lady Macduff with her children, a single line of antagonism builds up through Malcolm and Fleance to the effectual revenger, Macduff. There is evidence, in the original text and in the subsequent stage-history, to show that the grim spareness of the plot was eked out by additional grotesqueries on the part of the Witches.

I make this preliminary obeisance to the centrality of the hero-villain because it is not to him that I shall be calling your attention, though it should be evident already that he will be reflected upon by my sidelights. In skipping over the poetry of his speeches or the moral and psychological dimensions of character, I feel somewhat like the visitor to a Gothic edifice whose exclusive focus is devoted to a gargoyle here and there. I should not be doing so if the monument as a whole were less memorably familiar than it is, or if the artistic coherence of a masterpiece did not so frequently reveal itself through the scrutiny of an incidental detail. My two short texts are quite unevenly matched, though not disconnected in the long run. One of them, the Porter's Scene, has been regarded more often than not as a mere excrescence or intrusion. The other, the Sleepwalking Scene, has become one of the high spots in the repertory as a set piece for distinguished actresses. The lowest common denominator between them is that both have been written in prose. Apart from more functional purposes, such as documents and announcements, Shakespeare makes use of prose to convey an effect of what Brian Vickers terms "otherness," a different mode of diction from the norm. To cite the clearest instance, Hamlet's normal personality is expressed in blank verse; he falls into prose when he puts on his "antic disposition." This combines, as do the fools' roles, the two major uses of Shakespeare's non-metrical speech: on the one hand, comedy, low life, oftentimes both; on the other, the language of psychic disturbance.

Our two scenes are enacted in these two modes respectively. But, before we turn to them, let us take a very brief glance at the outdoor stage of the Shakespearean playhouse. On that subject there has been an infinite deal of specific conjecture over a poor halfpennyworth of reliable documentation, and many of those conjectures have disagreed with one another. Over its most general features, however, there is rough agreement, and that is all we need here. We know that its large jutting platform had a roof supported by two pillars downstage; one of which might conveniently have served as the tree where Orlando hangs his verses in *As You Like It*. We are also aware of an acting space "aloft" at stage rear, whence Juliet or Prospero could have looked down. As for the curtained space beneath, that remains an area of

veiled uncertainty. Yet the back wall of the tiring-house had
to include an outside doorway big enough to accommodate
the inflow and outflow of sizable properties, and possibly to
present a more or less literal gate upon due occasion. Hence
it is not difficult to conceive of the stage as the courtyard of
a castle, into which outsiders would arrive, and off of which
branched chambers for the guests, who might hurriedly rush
out from them if aroused by some emergency. Moreover,
the surrounding auditorium, open to the skies and rising in
three tiers of galleries, might itself have presented a kind of
courtyard. Not that this arrangement was representational.
It was the stylization of the theatrical arena that made possible its scope and adaptability.

Much depended, of course, upon the convention of verbal scenery. When the aged, gracious, and serene King
Duncan appears at the gate of Glamis Castle, his introduc-
tory words sketch the setting and suggest the atmosphere:

(I, vi, 1–
3)*

> This castle hath a pleasant seat, the air
> Nimbly and sweetly recommends itself
> Unto our gentle senses.

The description is amplified by Banquo with his mention of
"the temple-haunting marlet," the bird whose presence almost seems to consecrate a church, one of the succession of
birds benign and malign whose auspices are continually in-
voked. The description of the marlet's "procreant cradle"
(8)—and procreation is one of the points at issue throughout—assures us that "the heaven's breath / Smells wooingly
here" (5,6). And Banquo completes the stage-design:

(9, 10)

> Where they most breed and haunt, I have observ'd
> The air is delicate.

Knowing what we have been informed with regard to Duncan's reception, and what he is so poignantly unaware of,
we may well find it a delicate situation. Stressing its contrast
to the episodes that precede and follow it, Sir Joshua Reyn-
olds called it "a striking instance of what in painting is
termed *repose*." Repose—or rather, the absence of it—is
fated to become a major theme of the tragedy. It will mean
not rest but restlessness for Macbeth, when Duncan all too

soon is accorded his last repose. Are we not much nearer, at this point, to the fumes of hell than to the heaven's breath? Macbeth, as he will recognize in a soliloquy, "should gainst his murtherer shut the door," rather than hypocritically welcoming Duncan in order to murder him (I, vii, 15). Duncan has been a ruler who exemplified royalty, a guest who deserved hospitality, and a man of many virtues who has commanded respect, as Macbeth himself acknowledges. The scene is set for the crimes and their consequences by this two-faced welcome into the courtyard of Macbeth's castle.

By the end of the incident-crowded First Act, in spite of his hesitant asides and soliloquies, everything has fallen into place for the consummation of the Witches' cackling prophecies. The Second Act begins ominously with Banquo's muted misgivings; he supplicates the "merciful powers"—who seem less responsive than those darker spirits addressed by Lady Macbeth—to restrain in him "the cursed thoughts that nature / Gives way to in repose," and retires after Macbeth has wished him "Good repose" (II, i, 7–9, 29). This exchange would seem to occur in the courtyard, which becomes the base of operations for the murder. The first scene culminates in the vision of the dagger, hypnotically drawing Macbeth to the door of Duncan's quarters. Leaving them after the deed, as he recounts to his wife in the second scene, he has experienced another hallucination: the voice that cried "Sleep no more!" (II, ii, 32). Meanwhile Lady Macbeth has soliloquized, fortified with drink, and he has cried out offstage at the fatal instant. One residual touch of humanity, the memory of her own father, has inhibited her from killing the king herself; but she is Amazonian enough, taking the bloody daggers from her badly shaken husband with a crude and cruel joke (the pun on "gild" and "guilt"), to reenter the death chamber and plant them upon the sleeping grooms (II, ii, 53–54). It is then that the tensely whispered colloquies between the guilty couple are suddenly interrupted by that most portentous of sound effects: the knocking at the gate.

This is the point of departure for a well-known essay by Thomas De Quincey, who argues, rather overingeniously, that the interruption helps to restore normality, calming the excited sensibilities of the spectator. "The reaction has commenced; the human has made its reflux upon the fiendish; the pulses of life are beginning to beat again," De Quincey concludes, "the reestablishment of the goings-on of the world in which we live makes us profoundly sensible of the awful parenthesis that had suspended them." Here De Quincey, who elsewhere styled himself "a connoisseur of murder," seems to have got his proportions wrong. Surely it is the Porter's Scene that forms a parenthesis in an increasingly awful train of events. "Every noise appalls me," Macbeth has said (II, ii, 55). For him—and for us as well—the knock reverberates with the menace of retribution, like the opening notes of Beethoven's Fifth Symphony. It heralds no resumption of diurnal business as usual. Let us bear in mind that the knocker is to be the avenger, the victim who will have suffered most from the tyrant's cruelty. Macduff's quarrel with Macbeth, according to Holinshed's chronicle, first arose because the Thane of Fife did not fully participate when commanded by the King of Scotland to help him build the new castle at Dunsinane. It is surprising that Shakespeare did not utilize that hint of motivation; possibly he did, and the scene was among those lost through the rigors of cutting. It would have added another turn of the screw to Macbeth's seizure of Macduff's castle at Fife and the domestic massacre therein.

As for Dunsinane Castle, it is ironic that Macbeth should count upon its strength and that it should be so easily surrendered, "gently rend'red," after a few alarums and excursions (V, vii, 24). It comes as a final reversal of the natural order that he, besieged and bound in, should be assaulted and overcome by what appears to be a walking forest. So, in the earlier scenes, the manifest presumption is that the pleasantly situated Glamis Castle would be a haven and a sanctuary, associated with temples by Macbeth as well as Banquo. Rapidly it proves to be the opposite for its guests, whereas those menacing thumps at the gateway announce the arrival not of a dangerous enemy but of their predestined ally. Despite his sacrifice and suffering, his quasi-miraculous birth, and his intervention on the side of the angels, I shall refrain from presenting Macduff as a Christ-figure. There are altogether too many of these in current literary criticism—many more, I fear, than exist in real life. Yet it is enlightening to consider the suggested analogy between this episode and that pageant in the mystery cycles which dramatizes the Harrowing of Hell. Some of those old guild-plays were still being acted during Shakespeare's boyhood; nearby Coventry was a center for them; and we meet with occasional allusions to them in Shakespeare's plays, notably to Herod whose furious ranting had made him a popular byword. Without the Slaughter of the Innocents, over which he presided, the horrendous slaughter at Macduff's castle would have been unthinkable. Many later audiences, which might have flinched, have been spared it.

When Jesus stands before the gates of hell, in the Wakefield cycle, his way is barred by a gatekeeper suggestively named Rybald, who tells his fellow devil Beelzebub to tie up those souls which are about to be delivered: "how, belsabub! bynde thise boys, / sich harow was never hard in hell." The command of Jesus that the gates be opened takes the form of a Latin cadence from the liturgy, *Attollite portas. . .* This, in turn, is based upon the vulgate phrasing of the Twenty-fourth Psalm: "Lift up your heads, O ye gates; even lift them up, ye everlasting doors; and the King of glory shall come in." The liturgical Latin echoes the rite of Palm Sunday celebrating Christ's entrance into Jerusalem. It was also chanted before the portals of a church during the ceremonies of consecration. In the mystery, Jesus enters hell to debate with Satan and ends by rescuing therefrom various worthies out of the Old Testament. That is the typological situation which prefigured Shakespeare's comic gag. We must now turn back to his dilatory Porter, after having kept the visitor waiting outside longer than the Porter will. Obviously the action is continuous between Scenes Two and Three, with the repeated knocking to mark the continuity. "Wake Duncan with thy knocking! I would thou couldst!" is the exit line (II, ii, 71). Macbeth, unnerved, is guided to their chamber by his wife, as he will be again in the Banquet

Scene, and as she will imagine in the Sleepwalking Scene. There should be a minute when the stage is bare, and the only drama is the knocking.

But it will take a longer interval for the couple to wash off the blood and change into night attire. This is the theatrical necessity that provides the Porter with his cue and one of the troupe's comedians with a small part. Shakespeare's clowns tend to be more stylized than his other characters, most specifically the fools created by Robert Armin, and probably to reflect the personal style of certain actors. Will Kemp, who preceded Armin as principal comedian, seems to have specialized in voluble servants. It may well have been Kemp who created the rather similar roles of Launce in *The Two Gentlemen of Verona* and Launcelot Gobbo in *The Merchant of Venice*. Each of these has his characteristic routine: a monologue which becomes a dialogue as the speaker addresses himself to imagined interlocutors. Gobbo's is especially apropos, since it pits his conscience against the fiend. Shakespeare did not abandon that vein after Kemp left the company; indeed he brought it to its highest pitch of development in Falstaff's catechism on honor. The Porter's little act is pitched at a much lower level, yet it can be better understood in the light of such parallels. The sleepy Porter stumbles in, bearing the standard attributes of his office, a lantern and some keys. He is not drunk now; but, like others in the castle, he has been carousing late; and his fantasy may be inspired by the penitential mood of the morning after. "If a man were Porter of Hell Gate"—that is the hypothesis on which he is ready to act—"he should have old turning the key"—he should have to admit innumerable sinners (II, iii, 1–3).

An audience acquainted with Marlowe's *Doctor Faustus* would not have to be reminded that the hellmouth had figured in the mysteries. And the dramatist who had conceived the Brothel Scene in *Othello* had envisioned a character, namely Emilia, who could be accused of keeping—as the opposite number of Saint Peter—"the gate of hell" (IV, ii, 92). The Porter assumes that stance by choice, asking himself: "Who's there, i' th' name of Belzebub?" (3–4). He answers himself by admitting three social offenders. It has been his plan, he then confides, to have passed in review "all professions," doubtless with an appropriately satirical comment on each (18). But, despite the histrionic pretence that hellfire is roaring away, the Porter's teeth are chattering in the chill of early morning: "this place is too cold for hell" (16–17). Neither the time-serving farmer nor the hose-stealing tailor seems as pertinent a wrongdoer as the equivocator, "who could not equivocate to heaven" (10–11). Here the editors digress to inform us about the trial and execution of Henry Garnet, Superior of the Jesuit Order, in 1606. The topical allusion is helpful, insofar as it indicates how the word came to be in the air; and Garnet's casuistry had to do with treason and attempted regicide, the notorious Gunpowder Plot. But *Macbeth* is not exactly a satire on the Jesuits. Maeterlinck, in his translation, renders "equivocator" by "*jésuite*" because there is no cognate French equivalent. The thematic significance of the Porter's speech lies in its anticipation of the oracles ("these juggling fiends"), which turn out to be true in an unanticipated sense: "th' equivocation of the fiend" (V, viii, 19; V, v, 42).

The Porter, who has been parrying the knocks by echoing them, finally shuffles to the gate, lets in Macduff and Lenox, and stands by for his tip: "I pray you remember the porter" (20–21). Drink, which has inebriated the grooms and emboldened Lady Macbeth, is his poor excuse for tardiness. The after-effects of drinking are the subject of his vulgar and not very funny riddle: "nose-painting, sleep, and urine" (28). Then, licensed perhaps by the precedent of the devil-porter Rybald, he moves on to the equivocal subject of lechery. If drink provokes the desire but takes away the performance, it is a paradigm for Macbeth's ambition. For, as Lady Macbeth will realize: "Nought's had, all's spent, / Where our desire is got without content" (III, ii, 4–5). When liquor is declared to be "an equivocator with lechery," that equivocation is demonstrated by the give-and-take of the Porter's rhythms: "it makes him, and it mars him; it sets him on, and it takes him off; it persuades him, and disheartens him; makes him stand to, and not stand to; in conclusion, equivocates him in a sleep, and giving him the lie, leaves him" (II, iii, 32–36). Each of these paired clauses, here again, links a false promise with a defeated expectation, expiring into drunken slumber after a moment of disappointed potency. The see-saw of the cadencing is as much of a prophecy as the Witches' couplets, and it has the advantage of pointing unequivocally toward the dénouement. The repartee trails off, after a lame pun about lying, with the reentrance of Macbeth, for which the Porter has been gaining time by going through his turn.

That turn has regularly been an object of expurgation, both in the theater and in print. I am not digressive if I recall that, when I wrote the introduction to a school-edition several years ago, the publishers wanted to leave out the Porter's ribaldry. I insisted upon an unbowdlerized text; but their apprehensions were commercially warranted; the textbook, though it is in a well-known series, has hardly circulated at all. Thousands of adolescents have been saved from the hazards of contemplating alcoholism, sex, and micturition. On a higher critical plane—some would say the highest—Coleridge was so nauseated by the whole scene that he ruled it out of the canon, declaring that it had been "written for the mob by another hand." The sentence about "the primrose way to th' everlasting bonfire," Coleridge conceded, had a Shakespearean ring (II, iii, 19). Without pausing to wonder whether it might have been echoed from *Hamlet*, he characteristically assumed that Shakespeare himself had interpolated it within the interpolation of his unknown collaborator. This enabled him to beg the question with Coleridgean logic and to comment further on "the entire absence of comedy, nay, even of irony . . . in *Macbeth*." Wholly apart from the comedy or the authenticity of the Porter Scene, it must strike us as singularly obtuse to overlook the fundamental ironies of the play: its ambiguous predictions, its self-destructive misdeeds. It could be urged, in Coleridge's defense, that the concept of dramatic irony had not yet been formulated. Kierkegaard's thesis on it was published in 1840, having been anticipated by Connop Thirlwall just a few years before.

Coleridge's rejection is sustained by another high literary authority. In Schiller's German adaptation, the Porter is high-minded and cold sober. He has stayed awake to keep guard over the King, and therefore over all Scotland, as he tells Macbeth in an ambitious jest. Instead of masquerading as an infernal gatekeeper, he has sung a pious hymn to the sunrise and has ignored the knocking in order to finish his *Morgenlied*. Yet, for a century now, the current of opinion has run the other way; commentators have held, with J. W. Hales, that Shakespeare's Porter was authentic and by no means inappropriate. Robert Browning heartily agreed, and Bishop Wordsworth even allowed that the scene could be read with edification. So it should be, given its eschatological overtones. We have long discarded the neo-classical inhibitions regarding the intermixture of tragic and comic elements. We have learned, above all from Lear's Fool, that the comic can intensify the tragic, rather than simply offer itself as relief. Those "secret, black, and midnight hags," the Witches, who for Holinshed were goddesses of destiny, come as close as anything in Shakespeare to the chorus of Greek tragedy (IV. i. 48). But their outlandish imminence seems elusive and amoral because of their mysterious connection with the machinery of fate. The Porter's role is grotesquely choric in another sense. Like the Gardener in *Richard II*, he stands there to point the moral, to act out the object-lesson. This castle, far from reaching up toward heaven, is located at the brink of hell. Even now its lord has damned himself eternally.

Damnation is portended by the curse of sleeplessness, which has been foreshadowed among the spells that the First Witch proposed to cast upon the sea-captain: "Sleep shall neither night nor day / Hang upon his penthouse lid" (I, iii, 19–20). No sooner has the King been murdered than Macbeth hears the voice crying "Sleep no more!" and begins to extoll the blessing he has forfeited. The word itself is sounded thirty-two times, more than in any other play of Shakespeare's. Repeatedly sleep is compared with death. Almost enviously, after complaining of the "terrible dreams" that afflict him nightly, Macbeth evokes the buried Duncan: "After life's fitful fever he sleeps well" (III, ii, 18, 23). When he breaks down at the Banquet Scene before the apparition of Banquo's ghost, it is Lady Macbeth who assumes command, discharges the guests, and leads her husband off to bed with the soothing words: "You lack the season of all natures, sleep" (III, iv, 140). It should be noted that she does not see the ghost or hear the voice, and that she skeptically dismisses the air-drawn dagger as a subjective phenomenon: "the very painting of your fear" (III, iv, 60). Unlike Macbeth, she has no intercourse with the supernatural forces. To be sure, she has called upon the spirits to unsex her, fearing lest she be deterred from murder by the milk—the feminine attribute—of human kindness. And from the outset it is he, not she, who feels and expresses that remorse she has steeled herself against, those "compunctious visitings of nature" (I, v, 45). When they ultimately overtake her, his insomnia will have its counterpart in her somnambulism.

In keeping with her aloofness from supernaturalism, Shakespeare's treatment of her affliction seems so naturalistic that it is now and then cited among the clinical cases in abnormal psychology. According to the seventeenth-century frame of reference, she may show the symptoms of melancholia or—to invoke theological concepts that still can grip the audiences of films—demonic possession. Psychoanalysis tends to diagnose her malady as a manifestation of hysteria, which compels her to dramatize her anxiety instead of dreaming about it, to reenact the pattern of behavior that she has tried so desperately to repress. Freud regarded this sleepwalker and her sleepless mate as "two disunited parts of a single psychical individuality," together subsuming the possibilities of reaction to the crime, and underlined the transference from his response to hers, from his hallucinations to her mental disorder. In more social terms, the closeness of their complementary relationship seems strongly reinforced by the sexual bond between them. Three of the exit-lines emphasize their going to bed together. Caroline Spurgeon and other interpreters of Shakespeare's imagery have noticed that the most recurrent metaphor in the play has to do with dressing and undressing, transposed sometimes into arming and disarming or crowning and uncrowning. The sense of intimacy is enhanced by the recollection that the nightgowns mentioned are dressing-gowns, that under the bedclothes no clothing of any sort was worn in that day; and nakedness exposed is one of the other themes (a recent film has welcomed the opportunity for presenting a heroine in the nude). Lady Macbeth, as M. C. Bradbrook has observed, must have been a siren as well as a fury.

Inquiries into her motives have dwelt upon her childlessness, after having borne a child who evidently died, and that frustration seems to have kindled Macbeth's hostility toward the families of Banquo and Macduff. Deprived of happy motherhood, she takes a somewhat maternal attitude toward her spouse, and she seeks a vicarious fulfillment in her ruthless ambitions for his career. Holinshed had stressed her single-minded goading-on of her husband, "burning in unquenchable desire to bear the name of a queen." She may be a "fiend-like queen" to Malcolm and other enemies, but the characterization is highly nuanced when we contrast it with the termagant queens of Shakespeare's earliest histories (V, ix, 35). Criticism ranges all the way from Hazlitt ("a great bad woman whom we hate, but whom we fear more than we hate") to Coleridge ("a woman of a visionary and daydreaming turn of mind"). Coleridge had re-created Hamlet in his own image, after all, and his Lady Macbeth might pose as a model for Madame Bovary. The variance in interpretations extends from Lamartine's "perverted and passionate woman" to Tieck's emphasis on her conjugal tenderness, which provoked the mockery of Heine, who envisages her billing and cooing like a turtle dove. She may not be "such a dear" as Bernard Shaw discerned in Ellen Terry's portrayal; but she encompasses most of these images, inasmuch as Shakespeare clearly understood the ambivalence of aggression and sympathy in human beings. Her emotions and Macbeth's are timed to a different rhythm. As he hardens into a fighting posture, and his innate virility reasserts itself, she softens into fragile femininity, and her insecurities come to the surface of her breakdown.

Distraction of the mind is rendered by Shakespeare in a pithy, terse, staccato idiom which might not inappropriately be termed distracted prose. Madness, along with all the other moods of English tragedy, had originally been conveyed through blank verse, as when Titus Andronicus "runs lunatic." So it was in Kyd's operatic *Spanish Tragedy*,

though the later and more sophisticated ragings of its hero
would be added by another hand in prose. The innovation
was Marlowe's: in the First Part of *Tamburlaine* the captive
queen Zabina goes mad over the death of her consort Baja-
zet, and before her suicide gives utterance to a short prose
sequence of broken thoughts. Her farewell line, "Make
ready my coach . . . ," must have given Shakespeare a suggestion for Ophelia. He seized upon this technique and developed it to the point where it became, in the phrase of
Laertes, "A document in madness, / Thoughts and remem-
brance fitted." Ophelia distributing flowers, like King Lear
distributing weeds, obsessively renews the source of grief.
Edgar in the guise of Tom o' Bedlam deliberately imitates
such language as does Hamlet when he simulates insanity.
Lear's Fool is exceptional, since he is both a jester and a
natural; yet, in that dual role, he may be looked upon as a
mediator between the comic and the distracted prose. And
in *King Lear* as a whole, in the interrelationship between
the Lear-Cordelia plot and the Gloucester-Edgar underplot,
we have our most highly wrought example of the two plots
running parallel. As a matter of dramaturgic tradition, that
parallel tended in the direction of parody.

Thus, in the Second Shepherds' Play at Wakefield, the
serious plot about the nativity is parodied by the sheep-
stealing underplot, since the lamb is an emblem of Jesus. In
the oldest English secular comedy, *Fulgens and Lucres*,
while two suitors court the mistress, their respective servants court the maid—probably the most traditional of all
comic situations, harking back as far as Aristophanes'
Frogs. In *Doctor Faustus* the clowns burlesque the hero's
conjurations by purloining his magical book and conjuring
up a demon. This has its analogue in *The Tempest*, where
the conspiracy against Prospero is burlesqued by the clown-
ish complot. Having defended the essential seriousness of
the Porter's Scene, I am not moving toward an argument
that there is anything comic *per se* in the Sleepwalking
Scene; but there is something distinctly parodic about the
virtual repetition of a previous scene in such foreshortened
and denatured form. Murder will out, as the old adage cau-
tions; the modern detective story operates on the assumption

that the murderer returns to the locality of the crime. Lady Macbeth, always brave and bold when her husband was present, must sleep alone when he departs for the battlefield. It is then that her suppressed compunction, her latent sense of guilt, wells up from the depths of her subconscious anguish. Under the cover of darkness and semi-consciousness, she must now reenact her part, going through the motions of that scene in the courtyard on the night of Duncan's assassination, and recapitulating the crucial stages of the entire experience.

When the late Tyrone Guthrie staged his production at the Old Vic, he directed his leading lady, Flora Robson, to reproduce the exact gesticulation of the murder scene. Such an effect could not have been achieved within the Piranesi-like setting designed by Gordon Craig, where the sleepwalking was supposed to take place on the steps of a sweeping spiral staircase. One of the most theatrical features of this episode, however it be played, lies in the choreographic opportunity that it offers to the actress and the director. At the Globe Playhouse the principal problem in staging would have been the glaring fact that plays were performed there in broad daylight. That was simply met by a convention, which has been uncovered through the researches of W. J. Laurence. A special point was made of bringing out lanterns, tapers, or other lights, paradoxically enough, to indicate the darkness. But the lighting of the Sleepwalking Scene is not merely conventional. Lady Macbeth, we learn, can no longer abide the dark. "She has light by her continually," her Waiting Gentlewoman confides to the Doctor (V, i, 22–23). It is the candle she carries when she enters, no mere stage property either, throwing its beams like a good deed in a naughty world. Banquo, on a starless night, has referred metaphorically to the overclouded stars as extinguished candles. Macbeth, when the news of his wife's suicide is subsequently brought to him, will inveigh against the autumnal prospect of meaninglessness ahead, and the yesterdays behind that have "lighted fools / The way to dusty death" (V, v, 22–23). Life itself is the brief candle he would now blow out.

Lady Macbeth presumably carried her candle throughout

the scene until the London appearance of Sarah Siddons in 1785. She was severely criticized for setting it down on a table, so that she could pantomime the gesture of rubbing her hands. Sheridan, then manager of the Drury Lane, told her: "It would be thought a presumptuous innovation." Man of the theater that he was, he congratulated her upon it afterwards. But many in the audience were put off by it, and even more by her costume. She was wearing white satin, traditionally reserved for mad scenes, and later on would shift to a shroud-like garment. Mrs. Siddons as Lady Macbeth became, by wide consent, the greatest English actress in her greatest role. Hence we have a fair amount of testimony about her performance. A statuesque figure whose rich voice ranged from melancholy to peevishness, subsiding at times into eager whispers, she was "tragedy personified" for Hazlitt, who reports that "all her gestures were involuntary and mechanical." More physically active than her candle-burdened predecessors, who seem to have mainly glided, she excelled particularly at stage-business. The hand-rubbing was accompanied by a gesture of ladling water out of an imaginary ewer. When she held up one hand, she made a face at the smell—a bit of business which Leigh Hunt considered "unrefined." Yet, after she had made her exit stalking backwards, one witness testified: "I swear that I smelt blood!" She herself has attested that, when as a girl of twenty she began to study the part, she was overcome by a paroxysm of terror.

Turning more directly to "this slumb'ry agitation," we are prepared for it by the expository conversation between the Gentlewoman and the Doctor (V, i, 11). Lady Macbeth's twenty lines will be punctuated by their whispering comments. It is clear that there have been earlier visitations, and that Lady Macbeth has engaged in writing during one of them; but what she spoke the Gentlewoman firmly refuses to disclose. The Doctor, who has been watching with her during the last two nights, has so far witnessed nothing. But, from the account, he knows what to expect: "A great perturbation in nature, to receive at once the benefit of sleep and do the effects of watching!" (9–11). Sleep seems scarcely a benefit under the circumstances, much as it may be longed for by the watchful, the ever-wakeful Macbeth; and, though Lady Macbeth is actually sleeping, she is not only reliving the guilty past but incriminating herself. When she appears, the antiphonal comment ("You see her eyes are open." / "Ay, but their sense is shut.") raises that same question of moral blindness which Shakespeare explored in *King Lear* (24–25). If she could feel that her hands were cleansed when she washed them, her compulsive gesture would be a ritual of purification. Yet Pilate, washing his hands before the multitude, has become an archetype of complicity. Her opening observation and exclamation ("Yet here's a spot" . . . "Out, damn'd spot!") is a confession that prolonged and repeated ablutions have failed to purge her sins (31, 35). She continues by imagining that she hears the clock strike two: it is time for the assassination. Her revulsion from it compresses into three words all the onus of the Porter's garrulous commentary: "Hell is murky" (36).

That sudden glimpse of the bottomless pit does not keep her from the sanguinary course she has been pursuing. But the grandiose iambic pentameter of her courtyard speeches, inspiriting and rebuking her reluctant partner, has been contracted into a spasmodic series of curt, stark interjections, most of them monosyllabic. "Yet who would have thought the old man to have had so much blood in him?" (39–40). She had thought at least of her father, and had momentarily recoiled. Macbeth had feared that the deed might not "trammel up the consequence," might open the way for retributive counteraction, and indeed Duncan's blood has clamored for a terrible augmentation of bloodshed, has set off the chain-reaction of blood-feuds involving Banquo's progeny and Macduff's. Hitherto we had not been aware of Lady Macbeth's awareness of the latter, much less of how she might respond to his catastrophe. Her allusion to Lady Macduff seems reduced to the miniature scale of a nursery rhyme ("The Thane of Fife / had a wife"), but it culminates in the universal lamentation of *ubi est*: "Where is she now?" Then, more hand-washing, more conjugal reproach. Her listeners are realizing, more and more painfully, that they should not be listening; what she says should not be heard, should not have been spoken, should never have happened. "Here's the

smell of the blood still" (50). The olfactory metaphor has a
scriptural sanction, as Leigh Hunt should have remembered:
evil was a stench in righteous nostrils, and the offence of
Claudius smelled to heaven. The heartcry comes with the
recognition that the smell of blood will be there forever:
"All the perfumes of Arabia will not sweeten this little
hand" (50–51).

She had been clear-headed, tough-minded, and matter-
of-fact in tidying up after the murder: "A little water clears
us of this deed." It was Macbeth, exhausted and conscience-
stricken after his monstrous exertion, who had envisioned
its ethical consequences in a hyperbolic comparison:

> Will all great Neptune's ocean wash this blood
> Clean from my hand? No; this my hand will rather
> The multitudinous seas incarnadine,
> Making the green one red.

(II, ii, 57–60)

Her hand is smaller than his, and so—relatively speaking—
is her hyperbole. All the perfumes of Arabia, all the oil-
wells of Arabia, could not begin to fill the amplitude of the
ocean, and the contrast is completed by the oceanic swell of
his Latinate polysyllables. She has come to perceive, un-
willingly and belatedly, that the stigmata are irremovable.
He had perceived this at once and, moreover, reversed his
magniloquent trope. Never can the bloodstain be cleansed
away; on the contrary, it will pollute the world. No one can,
as she advised in another context, "lave our honors" (III, ii,
33). The sound that voices this perception on her part ("O,
O, O!'") was more than a sign when Mrs. Siddons voiced it,
we are told (V, i, 52). It was "a convulsive shudder—very
horrible." The one-sided marital dialogue goes on, reverting
to the tone of matter-of-factness. "Wash your hands, put on
your nightgown, look not so pale" (62–63). If Duncan is in
his grave, as Macbeth has mused, is not Banquo in a similar
condition? Where is he now? Reminiscence here reverberates from the Banquet Scene: "I tell you yet again, Banquo's
buried; he cannot come out on's grave" (63–64). These in-
ternalized anxieties that will not be so coolly exorcized are
far more harrowing than the externalized ghosts that beset

Richard III on the eve of battle. Having resumed his sol-
dierly occupation and been reassured by the Witches' au-
guries, Macbeth has put fear behind him, whatever the other
cares that are crowding upon him. It is therefore through
Lady Macbeth that we apprehend the approach of nemesis.

And then her terminal speech: "To bed, to bed; there's
knocking at the gate" (66–67). It is imaginary knocking;
what we hear again is silence, a silence powerful enough to
resurrect the encounter between those harbingers of revenge
and damnation, Macduff and the Porter. Her fantasy concludes by repeating what we have already watched in both
the Murder Scene and the Banquet Scene, when she led her
faltering husband offstage. "Come, come, come, come,
give me your hand" (67). Her next and penultimate remark
harks back to the concatenation of earlier events. The First
Witch, in her premonitory resentment against the sailor's
wife, had promised him a swarm of nameless mischiefs (future tense): "I'll do, I'll do, and I'll do" (I, iii, 10). Macbeth's own ruminations at the edge of action had started
from the premise (present tense, conditional and indicative):
"If it were done, when 'tis done, then 'twere well / It were
done quickly" (I, vii, 1–2). It was done quickly, whereupon
Lady Macbeth sought to arrest his mounting disquietude
with the flat affirmation (past, transitive): "What's done, is
done" (III, ii, 12). Similar as it sounds, it was a far cry from
her concluding negation, her fatalistic valediction to life:
"What's done cannot be undone" (V, i, 68). This implies the
wish that it had not been done, reinforces Macbeth's initial
feeling that it need not be done, and equilibrates the play's
dialectical movement between free will and inevitability.
The appeal, "To bed," is uttered five times. She moves off
to the bedchamber they will never share again, as if she still
were guiding her absent husband's steps and his bloodstained hand were still in hers.

The doctor, who has been taking notes, confesses himself
to be baffled. The case is beyond his practise, it requires a
divine rather than a physician. In the following scene he
discusses it with Macbeth on a more or less psychiatric basis. Lady Macbeth is "Not so sick . . . / As she is troubled

with thick-coming fancies, / That keep her from her rest"
(V, iii, 37–39). The Doctor is not a psychiatrist; he cannot
"minister to a mind diseas'd" (40). Nor has he a cure for
Scotland's disease, when Macbeth rhetorically questions
him. Here we catch the connection with the one scene that
passes in England, where the dramatic values center on
Macduff's reaction to his domestic tragedy. His interview
with Malcolm is a test of loyalty, and the invented accusa-
tions that Malcolm levels against himself—that he would,
for instance, "Pour the sweet milk of concord into hell"—
are more applicable to Macbeth, whose milky nature has
gone just that way (IV, iii, 98). We are at the court of Edward the Confessor, the saintly English king whose virtues
make him a foil for the Scottish hellhound. A passage which
might seem to be a digression expatiates on how the royal
touch can cure his ailing subjects of the scrofula, known
accordingly as the King's Evil. Shakespeare is compliment-
ing the new Stuart monarch, James I, descendant of the leg-
endary Banquo, who had revived the ancient superstition.
But the pertinence goes further; for the spokesman of the
English king is another doctor; and the antithesis is brought
home when we compare the sickness of the one country
with that of the other. The King's Evil? Given the omens,
the tidings, the disaffections, is it not Scotland which suffers
from that disease?

A. C. Bradley asserted that Lady Macbeth is "the only
one of Shakespeare's great tragic characters who on a last
appearance is denied the dignity of verse." That comment
discloses a curious insensitivity not only to the ways of the
theater, which never interested Bradley very much, but to
the insights of psychology, for which he claimed an especial
concern. It could be maintained that distracted prose consti-
tutes an intensive vein of poetry. Somnambulism, though
fairly rare as a habit among adults (much rarer than sleep-
talking), is such a striking one that we might expect it to
have had more impact upon the imagination. Yet there
seems to be little or no folklore about it, if we may judge
from its omission in Stith Thompson's comprehensive *In-
dex*. It has suggested the rather silly libretto of Bellini's op-

era, *La Sonnambula* (based upon a vaudeville-ballet by Scribe), where the sleepwalking heroine compromises herself by walking into a man's room at an inn, and then redeems her reputation by singing a coloratura aria while perambulating asleep on a rooftop. Dissimilarly, Verdi's *Macbetto* avoids such pyrotechnical possibilities. The prima donna, in her sleepwalking *scena*, sticks fairly close to Shakespeare's disjointed interjections, though her voice mounts to a Verdian lilt at the high point:

> Arabia intera
> rimandar sí piccol mano
> co' suoi balsami non puó,
> no, no, non puó . . .

The only serious dramatization that I can recall, apart from Shakespeare's, is Kleist's *Prinz Friedrich von Homburg*. In contradistinction to Lady Macbeth, Prince Friedrich has already made his promenade when the play opens; he is discovered at morning seated in a garden; and the garland he is unconsciously weaving adumbrates his dreams of future military glory. The title of Hermann Broch's fictional trilogy, *Die Schlafwandler*, is purely figurative. A melodrama made famous by Henry Irving, *The Bells*, culminates in the mesmerized reenactment of a crime. It is worth noting that the first *Macbeth* acted in German (1773), freely adapted by Gottlob Stefanie der Jüngere, replaced the sleepwalking scene by a mad scene in which Macbeth was stabbed to death by his lady. Shakespeare would seem to have been as unique in his choice of subject as in his handling of it.

There is nothing to prevent a mad scene from taking place in the daytime. But Lady Macbeth must be a noctambulist as well as a somnambulist, for her climactic episode brings out the nocturnal shading of the tragedy. *Macbeth*, from first to last, is deeply and darkly involved with the night-side of things. Both Macbeth and Lady Macbeth apostrophize the darkness, calling upon it to cover their malefactions. The timing of crucial scenes is conveyed, not merely by the convention of lighting candles, but by the recurring imagery of nightfall, overcast and dreamlike as in the dagger speech:

(II, i, 49–51)

>   Now o'er the one half world
>   Nature seems dead, and wicked dreams abuse
>   The curtain'd sleep.

Characters, habitually undressing or dressing, seem to be either going to bed or getting up, like the Porter when he is so loudly wakened. "Light thickens," and the mood can be summed up by the protagonist in a single couplet:

(III,   ii, 52–53)

>   Good things of day begin to droop and drowse,
>   Whiles night's black agents to their preys do rouse.

Critical decisions are reached and fell designs are carried out at hours when night is "Almost at odds with morning, which is which," when the atmosphere—like hell—is murky, and it is hard to distinguish fair from foul or foul from fair (III, iv, 126). The penalty for wilfulness is watchfulness, in the sense of staying awake against one's will, of fitfully tossing and turning between bad dreams. Existence has become a watching, a waking, a walking dream. Yet "night's predominance," as one of the Thanes describes it, cannot last forever (II, iv, 8). Malcolm offers consolation by saying: "The night is long that never finds the day" (IV, iii, 240). Macduff is fated to bring in the head of Macbeth on a pike, like the Thane of Cawdor's at the beginning, and to announce the good word: "the time is free" (V, ix, 21). The human makes its reflux over the fiendish at long last. After so painful and protracted an agony, after a spell so oneiric and so insomniac by turns, we welcome the daylight as if we were awakening from a nightmare.

The Poetry of the Lyric Group: *Richard II*, *Romeo and Juliet*, *A Midsummer Night's Dream*

4

HALLETT SMITH

A year ago I gave the Third Annual Shakespeare Lecture to the Shakespeare Association of America. In it I dealt mainly with two topics: the apparent intrusion of poetry into some of Shakespeare's plays at points where one would expect dramatic, rather than lyrical, writing; and the extraction, over the years, by anthologists, of poetic passages from the plays. The subtitle of my lecture was intended to be partly jocular, partly serious. It was "What are the Beauties of Shakespeare Doing in Shakespeare?"

Now I am interested in focusing more narrowly on the general question of the poet-playwright: does he suppress something in himself when he struggles to master the difficult craft of writing plays which will succeed on the stage? Or, perhaps more interestingly, can we detect and appreciate those points at which he did not succeed in suppressing the poet in him? There is a long list of poets in the nineteenth century, and the twentieth, too, for that matter, who tried to make themselves into playwrights and didn't succeed. Perhaps it's just as well.[1]

But Shakespeare certainly did succeed in becoming a master craftsman in the theater, and most Shakespeare scholarship these days quite properly concerns itself with the nature of his craft or with the intellectual background of his plays. I am looking in quite the opposite direction. I

---

1. One should bear in mind F. P. Wilson's comment on the famous lines in Marlowe's *Tamburlaine* beginning "If all the pens that poets ever held": "To those who say that this poetry is undramatic I would answer that no poetry is undramatic that brings all sorts and conditions of men into the theatre and forces them to listen." *Marlowe and the Early Shakespeare* (Oxford: Clarendon Press, 1953), p. 35.

have heard it said that the way to make a lot of money in the stock market is to observe what everybody else is doing and then do the opposite. I have never had the opportunity to try that out, and I would probably be afraid to anyway, but in Shakespeare studies there is something to be said for walking on the side of the road in the opposite direction to the heavy traffic.

Therefore I propose to consider the nature of the poetry in three plays, and, to make the job as easy for myself as I can, I have chosen the plays that are sometimes called "the lyrical group"—*Richard II*, *Romeo and Juliet* and *A Midsummer Night's Dream*. There is a great deal of poetry in each of these plays, and a lecture might well devote itself to only one of them, or indeed, to only part of one. I suppose I am surveying instead of digging.

The richness of the poetry here has not always met with approval of the critics. T. S. Eliot, himself a poet who turned to writing plays, remarked that "the self-education of a poet trying to write for the theatre seems to require a long period of disciplining his poetry, and putting it, so to speak, on a very thin diet."[2] And forty years ago Richard David, in a little book called *The Janus of Poets*, wrote: "It is possible to be too poetical for drama . . . even Shakespeare, at least in his early plays, may be accused of prolonging his lyricism further than the situation gives any warrant for."[3] These remarks may not be specifically directed at *Richard II*, but Travis Bogard says that "in *Richard II*, Shakespeare first became himself."[4] And so, with that play will I first begin.

Shakespeare was certainly familiar with Marlowe's *Edward II*. This declaration, on which there is no disagreement, is endorsed by Geoffrey Bullough, though he does

2. *Poetry and Drama* (Cambridge, Mass.: Harvard University Press, 1951), p. 32. Eliot goes on to say that "there may be a later stage, when (and if) the understanding of theatrical technique has become second nature, at which he can dare to make more liberal use of poetry and take greater liberties with ordinary colloquial speech. I base that belief on the evolution of Shakespeare and on some study of the language in his late plays."

3. P. xi.

4. "Shakespeare's Second Richard," *PMLA* 70 (1955): 193.

not print *Edward II* among his "Sources" or "Possible Sources." A number of analyses of the two plays have been made, but none, I think, has sufficiently stressed the poetry of Marlowe's play. A recent production of it on television almost completely smothered the poetry, so I remind you of the words Edward speaks to Lightborn at the end:

> *K. Edw:* Weepst thou already? list awhile to me
> And then thy heart, were it as Gurney's is,
> Or as Matrevis', hewn from Caucasus,[5]
> Yet will it melt, ere I have done my tale.
> This dungeon where they keep me is the sink
> Wherein the filth of all the castle falls.
>
> ....
>
> And there in mire and puddle have I stood
> This ten days' space; and, lest that I should sleep,
> One plays continually upon a drum.
> They give me bread and water, being a king,
> So that, for want of sleep and sustenance,
> My mind's distempered, and my body's numb'd,
> And whether I have limbs or not I know not.
> O, would my blood dropp'd out from every vein,
> As doth this water from my tattered robes.
> Tell Isabel, the Queen, I look'd not thus,
> When for her sake I ran at tilt in France
> And there unhors'd the duke of Cleremont.
>
> *(V, v, 51–69)*

Whatever else it is, that is magnificent poetry, and it must have stimulated Shakespeare. He doesn't so much imitate Marlowe, W. B. C. Watkins observed,[6] as consciously improve upon him. It may be that he had an ambition similar to that which Spenser had (according to Harvey), an ambition to "overgo Ariosto"; but to overgo Marlowe, who was closer and more obvious, was even more challenging. That does *not* mean that I think Marlowe was the Rival Poet of the Sonnets.

I will turn in a moment to Richard's final soliloquy, but first I must deal with a venerable notion that the reason

---

5. It is interesting that Shakespeare uses the Caucasus as a symbol for cold only once, in *Richard II* (I, iii, 295). All references to and quotations from Shakespare's works are from *The Riverside Shakespeare* (1974).

6. *Shakespeare and Spenser* (Princeton, N. J.: Princeton University Press, 1950), p. 77.

Richard fails is that he is a poet. This view gets its clearest, though by no means its earliest, expression from Mark Van Doren. According to him, the power Shakespeare discovered in himself "is one that makes himself conscious of himself as a poet. It is the power to write the English language musically—with a continuous melody and with unfailing reserves of harmony. His king will be similarly self-conscious; that will explain the sympathy between the author and his creation, as well as provide the author an opportunity to criticize his own excesses in an extension of himself. For Richard will not become a great poet. Merely 'musical' poets seldom do. But the great poet of the play is Richard. And if he has to content himself with being a minor poet, that circumstance is consistent with the character of the man and of the action built around him. The play is organized about a hero who, more indeed than contenting himself with the role of minor poet, luxuriates in it. His theme is himself. He dramatizes his grief. He spends himself in poetry— which is something he loves more than power and more than any other person. His self-love is grounded upon an infatuation with the art he so proudly and self-consciously practices. That is what 'Richard II' is about and what even its plot expresses. Its unity therefore is distinct and impressive."[7]

This conception of Richard as a king who failed because he was a poet goes back, through F. S. Boas, to Dowden, and Nicholas Brooke has recently called this the "public school attitude," scornful of such effeminate things as poetry and dedicated to the manly virtues exhibited in team sports. But Madeleine Doran, Geoffrey Bullough, and others have pointed out that it is an error to suppose that Richard is a poet because he speaks lovely verse; so does Hotspur sometimes, though he despises poetry, and so does Caliban on occasion, though he says that the only benefit he got from language was that it enabled him to curse.

No, it is not so much that Richard II, the character, is full of poetry. One need not point to John of Gaunt's famous dying speech—the high-water mark of Little England sen-

7. *Shakespeare* (1942) p. 89.

timent—or Mowbray's passionate identification of our native language with the air we breathe. There is another passage which was characterized by Dr. Johnson as "in the
highest degree poetical and striking."[8] What would you expect Dr. Johnson to attach those words to? Something very
general, very abstract, very moral? Here is the passage:

> The bay-trees in our country are all wither'd,
> And meteors fright the fixéd stars of heaven,
> The pale-faced moon looks bloody on the earth,
> And lean-look'd prophets whisper fearful change,
> Rich men look sad, and ruffians dance and leap,
> The one in fear to lose what they enjoy,
> The other to enjoy by rage and war.
> These signs forerun the death or fall of kings.

These lines might conceivably have been written by Coleridge. But that is not my point. Who speaks them in Shakespeare? Why, a Welsh captain, who does nothing whatever
in the play, except to report to the Earl of Salisbury that
Richard's hoped-for support has fallen away.

The answer to the argument that Richard fails because he
is a poet is that *everybody* in the play is a poet: the widowed
Duchess of Gloucester, Bullingbrook as he refutes his
father's comforting advice at the time of his banishment, the
gardeners, that Welsh captain, and so on. It is well put by
Sir John Gielgud (the greatest Shakespearean actor of our
time, I take it, though I was once assured by an elderly
gentleman that he was surpassed by another knight, Sir
Johnston Forbes-Robertson, who retired in 1913):

"Unfortunately," says Gielgud, "throughout the tragedy,
the verse seems to be too evenly distributed, and often with
more music than sense of character. Everyone speaks in images, parentheses, and elaborate similes, whether gardeners, exquisites, or tough realistic nobles, and though this
richness of metaphor gives, in reading, a beautiful, tapes-
tried, somewhat Gothic effect (like an illuminated missal or
a Book of Hours), the continually artificial style tends to
become somewhat indigestible on the stage, and stands be-

8. *Johnson on Shakespeare*, vol. 7 in *The Yale Johnson*, ed. Arthur
Sherbo (New Haven: Yale University Press, 1968), p. 438.

tween the audience and their desire to get on more intimate
terms with the characters and situations."[9]

The actor may well feel hampered by the intrusion of
poetry. It is not so much that it is difficult to speak, though
it is so difficult that in my judgment very few modern actors
have mastered the art, but that, by Gielgud's testimony, it
dilutes that fine relationship between actor and audience
which is a high concentration of action and character. But
Shakespeare was himself an actor, remember, as well as a
poet and playwright, and his "quality," as the Elizabethans
called his profession, came to the forefront of his imagination when he had the Duke of York describe to his duchess
the entry of Richard after Bullingbrook into London:

> As in a theatre the eyes of men,
> After a well-graced actor leaves the stage,
> Are idly bent on him that enters next,
> Thinking his prattle to be tedious,
> Even so, or with much more contempt, men's eyes
> Did scowl on gentle Richard. No man cried "God save him!"
> No joyful tongue gave him his welcome home,
> But dust was thrown upon his sacred head,
> Which with such gentle sorrow he shook off,
> His face still combating with tears and smiles,
> The badges of his grief and patience,
> That had not God, for some strong purpose, steel'd
> The hearts of men, they must perforce have melted,
> And barbarism itself have pitied him.

(V, ii, 23–36)

Dryden, himself a poet and no stranger to the stage, said of
this passage "the painting of it is so lively, and the words so
moving, that I have scarce read anything comparable to it,
in any other language."

Much attention has been paid to the imagery in *Richard
II*, and valuable contributions have been made by Madeleine Doran, Wolfgang Clemen, and Richard Altick.[10] I

9. *Richard II: A Casebook*, ed. Nicholas Brooke (London: Macmillan,
1973), p. 79.
10. Madeleine Doran, "Imagery in *Richard II* and *Henry IV*" *MLR* 37
(1942):113–22; Wolfgang Clemen, *The Development of Shakespeare's
Imagery* (Cambridge, Mass.: Harvard University Press, 1951); Richard
D. Altick, "Symbolic Imagery in *Richard II*, " *PMLA* 62 (1947):339–65.

think it is important to see that the imagery is of different
kinds, as it is indeed in Shakespeare's sonnets, which I believe were mainly written about the time of these three lyrical plays, that is, in the mid-nineties. I will not here discuss
that whole thorny problem of the decorum to be followed in
selecting images, or the relationship of imagery to rhetorical
theory, which Rosemund Tuve sifted to the bran many years
ago. I will merely point to a few images and place them in
context with some from Shakespeare's contemporaries.
Marlowe's Edward, in a passage I have already quoted, says

> O, would my blood dropp'd out from every vein,
> As doth this water from my tattered robes.

Compare that with Richard's exclamation in his great scene
at the beginning of act IV, just before he calls for the mirror:

> O that I were a mockery king of snow,
> Standing before the sun of Bullingbrook,
> To melt myself away in water-drops!

Not only is Shakespeare's image far more complex, but the
verbal music of "mockery king" applied to the snowman,
the alliteration in the ironic phrase "standing before the sun
of Bullingbrook," and the marvelously eloquent conclusion
of "melting myself away in water-drops" is fully Shakespearean. A modern poet, Edith Sitwell, observes that here
"Grief and deprivation have the purity of snow, and its
light."

Another example points up the difference between
Shakespeare and Daniel, whose *Civil Wars* of 1595 he
surely knew. Here is Daniel:

> Thou sit'st at home safe by the quiet fire
> And hear'st of others harmes, but feelest none;
> And there thou tel'st of kinges and who aspire,
> Who fall, who rise, who triumphes, who doe mone:
> Perhappes thou talk'st of me, and dost inquire
> Of my restraint, why here I live alone,
> O know tis others sin, not my desart,
> And I could wish I were but as thou art.

And here is Shakespeare, in Richard's speech of farewell to
his queen:

In winter's tedious nights sit by the fire
With good old folks and let them tell [thee] tales
Of woeful ages long ago betid;
And ere thou bid good night, to quite their griefs,
Tell thou the lamentable tale of me
And send the hearers weeping to their beds.
For why, the senseless brands will sympathize
The heavy accent of thy moving tongue,
And in compassion weep the fire out,
(V, l, 40–   And some will mourn in ashes, some coal-black,
50)   For the deposing of a rightful king.

This passage resembles the last quatrain of Sonnet 73:

In me thou seest the glowing of such fire
That on the ashes of his youth doth lie,
As the death-bed whereon it must expire.
Consum'd with that which it was nourish'd by.

Shakespeare's manner in these lyrical passages is closer to
the limpid style of his songs than it is to allegory or to metaphysical poetry, but it is time to consider a passage which is
plainly allegorical, the garden scene. It is wholly Shakespeare's invention, of course; there is no hint of it in the
historical sources of the play. The idea that a country is like
a garden is of course an old *topos*, but, as Peter Ure says,
"The imaginative process most fundamental to the scene
was perhaps the granting of new life to an old metaphor, not
the borrowing of devices and sets of meanings from elsewhere. It was a response to a hidden force in language."[11]
Again, he speaks of it as "a dramatized parable."

The scene is, however didactic and moralizing, a daz-
zling display of poetry at work. Take the opening speech of
the gardener, and be aware of the fact that the gardener and
his man, presumably working-class people, speak verse,
not prose, and that the gardener opens with a simile:

Go bind thou up young dangling apricocks,
(III, iv,   Which like unruly children make their sire
29–31)   Stoop with oppression of their prodigal weight.

The quartos after the first read "yon dangling apricocks"

11. New Arden edition, 1956, p. lvi.

instead of "young," and the First Folio reads "yond." Shake-speare may have intended to write one of these, but he wrote "yong" and that generated the surprising idea of children making their parent "stoop with oppression of their prodigal weight." This gardener, as I have already suggested, is something of a poet, and even his helper, who presumably is not far up the social ladder, has at least a foot on the ascent to Parnassus, for he says, in a style reminiscent of John of Gaunt's famous speech,

> . . . our sea-walled garden, the whole land,
> Is full of weeds, her fairest flowers chok'd up,
> Her fruit-trees all unprun'd, her hedges ruin'd,
> Her knots disordered, and her wholesome herbs   *(III, iv,*
> Swarming with caterpillars . . .   *43–47).*

E. M. W. Tillyard quoted the opening lines of the gardener and then commented: "The first thought of a modern audience is: what a ridiculous way for a gardener to talk. The first thought of an Elizabethan would have been: what is the symbolic meaning of these words, spoken by the king of the garden, and how does it bear on the play?"[12] That sounds to me more like the first thought of a modern professor accustomed to making out examination questions than an ordinary member of an Elizabethan audience. At any rate, the audience would surely know that the queen and her women were overhearing, and that the conclusion of this would be one of poetic pathos, as indeed it is:

> *Gard:*   Poor queen, so that thy state might be no worse,
>   I would my skill were subject to thy curse.
>   Here did she fall a tear, here in this place
>   I'll set a bank of rue, sour herb of grace.
>   Rue, even for ruth, here shortly shall be seen,   *(III, iv,*
>   In the remembrance of a weeping queen.   *102–7)*

Robert Y. Turner's recent excellent book, *Shakespeare's Apprenticeship*, comments on the striking difference between *Richard II* and the earlier plays. Turner observes the presence of many dialogues about intimate emotions. "The sim-

---

12. In *Shakespeare: Modern Essays in Criticism*, ed. Leonard F. Dean, rev. ed. (New York: Oxford University Press, 1967), pp. 172–73.

plest of these new patterns," he says, "is the response of grief to saddening news. Almost the sole experience of Richard's queen on stage is to hear of misfortune. . . . The characters in *Richard II* not only talk about their feelings and sympathize with others but can remember their past, contradict themselves, intuit, and speculate on the future." [13] Clearly the mood of the play is one which can best be expressed in elegiac poetry.

One additional point about the poetry of *Richard II* demands attention. I refer again to Richard's soliloquy in prison and this time comment on its relationship to metaphysical poetry. Dame Helen Gardner has something to say about this, and there can, I suppose, be no more authoritative guide:

"Normally metaphor and simile," she says, "allow and invite the mind to stray beyond the immediate point of resemblance, and in extended or epic simile, which is the diametrical opposite of the conceit, the poet himself expatiates freely, making the point of comparison the point of departure. In an extended conceit, on the other hand, the poet forces fresh points of likeness upon us. Here the conceit is a kind of 'hammering out' by which a difficult join is made. I borrow the phrase from Shakespeare's poet-king Richard II, who occupies himself in prison composing a conceited poem. [Here she quotes the first six lines.] Longer conceits set themselves to 'prove' likeness. They may, as here, start from a comparison which the speaker owns is far from obvious and then proceeds to establish. Or they may start from one that is immediately acceptable and then make us accept further resemblances in detail after detail." She goes on to say that "A metaphysical conceit, unlike Richard's comparison of his prison to the world, is not indulged in for its own sake. It is used . . . to persuade, or it is used to define, or to prove a point." [14] There is, however, later in the soliloquy, a passage which might be, nay, has been, called metaphysical:

13. *Shakespeare's Apprenticeship* (Chicago: University of Chicago Press, 1974), pp. 27–30.
14. *The Metaphysical Poets*, ed. Helen Gardner, rev. ed. (London: Oxford University Press, 1967), pp. 19–20.

> Sometimes am I a king;
> Then treasons make me wish myself a beggar,
> And so I am. Then crushing penury
> Persuades me I was better when a king;
> Then am I king'd again, and by and by
> Think that I am unking'd by Bullingbrook,
> And straight am nothing. But what e'er I be,
> Nor I, nor any man that but man is,
> With nothing shall be pleas'd, till he be eas'd
> With being nothing.

(V, v, 32–41)

I think Parker Tyler has put it very well when he says "The something/nothing paradox needs only the religious affirmation to reproduce the metaphysical experience of the seventeenth century. . . . The metaphysical gesture is to re-create the world in terms of thought; thus, to imitate the act of divine creation."[15]

If I endorse this interesting idea I hope it will not be thought that in any way I approve of the most recent production of *Richard II* I have seen, in which Richard Chamberlain extended his arms in the death scene in such a way as to suggest very vividly the crucified Christ.

King Richard in his cruel prison meditates that anybody who is only a man will be pleased with nothing until he is eased out of life and become nothing. Shakespeare was fond of the theme: it is one of the great dramatic impulses of *King Lear*, both the character and the tragedy named after him. But that does not concern us here. We turn to another declaration about "nothing." It is Romeo's denunciation of Mercutio's highly poetic speech about Queen Mab. He was going on with it further, but Romeo interrupted him:

> Peace, peace, Mercutio, peace!
> Thou talk'st of nothing.

The nothing Romeo accused him of talking about was dreams; yet Romeo himself put great faith in dreams; that is how the subject came up. At the beginning of act V, Romeo says, in soliloquy,

---

15. "Phaethon: The Metaphysical Tension between the Ego and the Universe in English Poetry," *Accent* 16 (1956):34.

> If I may trust the flattering truth of sleep,
> My dreams presage some joyful news at hand.
> My bosom's lord sits lightly in his throne,
> And all this day an unaccustom'd spirit
> Lifts me above the ground with cheerful thoughts.

But perhaps the "nothing" Mercutio is accused of talking about is not so much dreams as poetry. For the Queen Mab speech is surely poetry. Coleridge, apparently depending upon this speech of just over forty lines, declared that "Mercutio is a man possessing all the elements of a poet: the whole world was, as it were, subject to his law of association. Whenever he wishes to impress anything, all things become his servants for the purpose: all things tell the same tale, and sound in unison."[16]

After Mercutio's disappearance from the scene, and the consequent killing of Tybalt by Romeo, the play changes direction. It begins, as Susan Snyder[17] has pointed out, with most of the characteristics of a comedy: Mercutio, a wit of the bawdy sort, a satirist of affected perfectionist fencers like Tybalt, a joker who attributes to Benvolio his own willingness to quarrel; the Nurse, garrulous and earthy, with ridiculous pretentions to dignity which are rendered hilarious when she tries to make a proper lady's serving man out of the clown Peter; old Capulet, the clearest example of a *senex iratus* in all of Shakespeare. But the death of Mercutio and the consequent death of Tybalt change all that.

Everyone has noticed that this play is full of antitheses, light and darkness, up and down, quick and slow, early and late, love and hatred. These give way to what Kenneth Muir calls "the finest poetry which had yet been heard on the English stage."[18] And Granville-Barker, considering the play from the point of view of producer, director, and actor, says "*Romeo and Juliet* is a lyric tragedy, and this must be the key to its interpreting."[19] Walter Pater called it a perfect

16. *Coleridge's Shakespearean Criticism*, ed. T. M. Raysor (Cambridge, Mass.: Harvard University Press 1930), 2:132.

17. "*Romeo and Juliet*: Comedy into Tragedy," *Essays in Criticism* 20 (1970):391–402.

18. *Shakespeare's Sources* (London: Methuen, 1957), p. 30.

19. *Prefaces to Shakespeare* (Princeton: Princeton University Press, 1947) 2:300.

symphony, and he praised especially Shakespeare's molding of three lyric forms, the sonnet, aubade, and the epithalamium, into a single harmonious whole.[20]

T. J. B. Spencer, in an earlier Tupper Memorial Shakespeare lecture, remarked that "It is perplexing that several of Shakespeare's great passages of poetry are not organic, or at least not obviously so. At times, certainly, he writes poetical 'set pieces' that are splendidly relevant. There are many in *Hamlet*, *Othello*, *King Lear*, and *The Tempest*, for example. But some highly wrought passages are not so easily spoken by the actor who has had to build up the 'character' from the action of the play."[21] He cites the Queen Mab speech as an example.

F. E. Halliday, in his book *The Poetry of Shakespeare's Plays*, would agree with Spencer: "Much of the verse spoken by Romeo and Juliet is pure lyric, bordering on the confines of music, love songs with so slender a dramatic significance that almost they might be abstracted from the play and applied to all young lovers whose tongues sound silver-sweet by night. Such verse makes little pretence to be dramatic, but sometimes verse that is intended to further the action forgets its function and slips into the same lyric vein."[22]

The opposition to this view is best expressed, I believe, by Moody Prior in his book on *The Language of Tragedy*. After noticing the different kinds of language used by the aristocrats Mercutio, Benvolio, and Romeo, and the Capulet servants who say things like "Where's Potpan, that he helps not to take away? He shift a trencher? He scrape a trencher?" he continues:

The sense of variety of treatment, however, is not the primary impression which the play leaves. It is the great brilliance and beauty of the speeches of the lovers and all that pertains to them which stands out most conspicuously. Moreover, in the diction of these speeches is to be found one of the principal features of order

20. *Richard II: A Casebook*, ed. Nicholas Brooke, p. 61.
21. "Shakespeare's Careless Art" In *Shakespeare's Art: Seven Essays*, ed. Milton Crane (Chicago: University of Chicago Press, 1973), pp. 129–30.
22. 1954. p. 78.

in the play. . . . Nothing could be more confusing, therefore, than to regard the big speeches, the familiar soliloquies, and the like, as lyrical interludes, or separable beauties, or to perpetuate as a legitimate critical necessity, as anything more than a temporary expedient, the distinction between Shakespeare the poet and Shakespeare the dramatist. Such a distinction can arise out of either too narrow a conception of the nature and function of drama, or too specialized a conception of the nature of poetry. In any case, it does violence to the remarkable unity of Shakespeare's art.[23]

Let us consider one of these speeches. It is at a critical point in the play. Romeo has just killed Tybalt and fled, exclaiming "O, I am fortune's fool!", the prince and the elder Montagues and Capulets have come to the scene, Juliet's mother refuses to believe Benvolio's accurate account of the fray and pleads:

(III, i,
180–1)
I beg for justice, which thou, Prince, must give:
Romeo slew Tybalt, Romeo must not live.

and the prince has exiled Romeo, with the standard defense of judicial severity: "Mercy but murders, pardoning those that kill." Juliet knows nothing of all this. She only knows that the Nurse will be coming soon with the rope ladder which will enable Romeo to reach her bedroom and consummate their marriage.

Gallop apace, you fiery-footed steeds,
Towards Phoebus' lodging; such a waggoner
As Phaëton would whip you to the west,
And bring in cloudy night immediately.
Spread thy close curtain, love-performing night,
That th' runaway's eyes may wink, and Romeo
Leap to these arms untalk'd of and unseen!
Lovers can see to do their amorous rites
By their own beauties, or, if love be blind,
It best agrees with night. Come, civil night,
Thou sober-suited matron all in black,
And learn me how to lose a winning match,
Play'd for a pair of stainless maidenhoods.
Hood my unmann'd blood, bating in my cheeks,

23. 1957, pp. 61–62, 74.

With thy black mantle, till strange love grow bold,
Think true love acted simple modesty.
Come night, come, Romeo, come, thou day in night,
For thou wilt lie upon the wings of night,
Whiter than new snow upon a raven's back.
Come, gentle night, come, loving, black-brow'd night,
Give me my Romeo, and, when I shall die,
Take him and cut him out in little stars,
And he will make the face of heaven so fine
That all the world will be in love with night,
And pay no worship to the garish sun.
O, I have bought a mansion of a love,
But not possess'd it, and, though I am sold,
Not yet enjoy'd. So tedious is this day
As is the night before some festival
To an impatient child that hath new robes
And may not wear them.   *(III, ii, 1–31)*

This is a serenade, an evening song; we are later to hear an
equally beautiful duet which is an aubade or morning song.
But just what kind of poetry is it? It invokes night, reversing
the classical and well-worn

> *O lente, lente, currite, noctes equi*

and evoking the whole Phaëton legend of the sun chariot
and the runaway horses. "Love-performing night" needs no
light to see by, except perhaps the light of the lovers' beauties. But love is "civil night, / Thou sober-suited matron all
in black," anticipating in a way Milton's *Il Penseroso*. It is
not always noticed how much modesty there is in the
speech. The passionate feelings, expressed very characteristically by Shakespeare in the imagery of hawking, are to
work in such a way that finally true love will be indistinguishable from simple modesty. Romeo is universalized by
being made a constellation after her (and, I suppose, his)
death,

> And he will make the face of heaven so fine
> That all the world will be in love with night,
> And pay no worship to the garish sun.

The theme of worship goes back to the first meeting of Romeo and Juliet at the ball, just as the image of hawking goes

back to the balcony scene. The next image, of a mansion acquired by a lord but not yet moved into, has caused some difficulty to the critics. That one's body is a mansion is commonplace; it is explicit in Sonnet 146 and elsewhere. The commercial images in the lines

O, I have bought a mansion of a love,
(III, ii,   But not possess'd it, and, though I am sold,
26–28)   Not yet enjoy'd.

are characteristically Shakespearean; the sonnets are full of them. But as generally astute and sensitive a critic as Nicholas Brooke has come to the conclusion that what these words mean is that Juliet has discovered that "in wanting her true love with Romeo she must experience the wish to be a whore in the fullest sense"![24] This must be one of the most fantastic of misreadings of Shakespeare. I return with relief to the common sense and practical theater experience of Granville-Barker. Speaking of Juliet, he says, "Not that there is anything of the budding sensualist in her; for to be sensual is to be sluggish, not fevered. Her passion for Romeo is ruled by imagination. And were this not the true reading of it, Shakespeare would have been all but compelled, one may say, to make it so; doubly compelled. Of what avail else would be his poetry, and through what other medium could a boy-actress realize the part? The beauty of the girl's story, and its agonies too, have imagination for their fount."[25]

More modern directors have trouble with Juliet's speech, because they do not realize the dramatic value of lyric poetry. According to one observer, "In Zeffirelli's production at the Old Vic in the 1950s, Juliet spoke this speech against a background of bells, bouncing up and down on her bed; the simple point was effectively made, of course, but everything else was missing. The words were quite inaudible, and she might well have done no more than say 'God! I feel randy!' "[26]

24. *Shakespeare's Early Tragedies* (London: Methuen, 1968), pp. 100–102.
25. *Prefaces to Shakespeare*, 2:344.
26. Brooke, *Shakespeare's Early Tragedies*, p. 86.

It will not be agreed by every critic of Shakespeare that *Richard II* is a tragedy, or indeed that *Romeo and Juliet* is a tragedy in the fullest sense. I have conceded that *Romeo and Juliet*, despite its dependence upon Arthur Brooke's lugubrious poem *Romeus and Juliet*, starts out like a comedy in many ways. But both these plays conform to a somewhat older conception of tragedy, the medieval notion that tragedy is a mere downfall or overthrow, as in Chaucer's *Monk's Tale*. I see a link between these two plays in a lament by Richard in which he says of himself:

>   Must he lose
> The name of king? a' God's name let it go.
> I'll give my jewels for a set of beads,
> My gorgeous palace for a hermitage,
> My gay apparel for an almsman's gown,
> My figur'd goblets for a dish of wood,
> My sceptre for a palmer's walking-staff,
> My subjects for a pair of carved saints   *(III, iii,*
> And my large kingdom for a little grave   *145–54)*

and in the lament of Old Capulet when he thinks his daughter dead:

> All things that we ordained festival,
> Turn from their office to black funeral:
> Our instruments to melancholy bells,
> Our wedding cheer to a sad burial feast;
> Our solemn hymns to sullen dirges change,
> Our bridal flowers serve for a buried corse;   *(IV, v,*
> And all things change them to the contrary.   *84–90)*

If the notion be accepted that *Richard II* is a history play developing toward tragedy, and that *Romeo and Juliet* is a tragedy which starts off as a comedy, despite a few warnings that the lovers are star-crossed and some fateful outcome hangs over them, there is no question at all that *A Midsummer Night's Dream* is a comedy. When, at the beginning of act V, Theseus is considering what kind of play shall be presented to the three pairs of lovers

> To wear away this long age of three hours   *(V, i, 33–*
> Between [our] after-supper and bed-time   *34)*

he is given a choice of heroic recital, the dramatization of a drunken riot (rejected because it is old hat, according to Theseus) and a satire, keen and critical, on the subject of the neglect of scholars by wealthy patrons and foundations; he chooses instead, against the advice of his master of the revels, a tedious brief scene of very tragical mirth.

Romeo and Juliet ends with the couplet

(V, iii,
309–10)

> For never was a story of more woe
> Than this of Juliet and her Romeo.

and I think we must agree that that is the prevailing tone of the play. On the contrary, *A Midsummer Night's Dream* is, in Thomas McFarland's phrase, "very possibly the happiest work of literature ever conceived."[27] If one reads (or sees) the three plays in the order I have suggested, he will notice that the first, *Richard II*, is the only one that has no prose in it, and very little, if any, comedy. The comic element increases as we go on to *Romeo and Juliet* and then to *A Midsummer Night's Dream*. It has long been recognized, also, that in a way the play of Pyramus and Thisbe has a close resemblance to the main story in *Romeo and Juliet*; it is burlesque because of the way the rude mechanicals discuss the technical problems of staging and characterization and because of the preposterous way in which they perform. But one can imagine them rehearsing a primitive form of *Romeo and Juliet* just as well, with Bottom offering to play Romeo, Mercutio, Juliet, or Tybalt—that might suit him as a "part to tear a cat in." Actually, of course, he develops in a way from Capulet's illiterate servant, the one who says, when he is handed a list of guests to invite to the ball,

27. *Shakespeare's Pastoral Comedy* (Chapel Hill: University of North Carolina Press, 1972), p. 78. My appreciation of *A Midsummer Night's Dream* has been greatly enhanced by Madeleine Doran's essays, "*A Midsummer Night's Dream*: A Metamorphosis," *Rice Institute Pamphlets* 46 (1960): 113–35, and "Titania's Wood," *Rice University Studies* 60 (1974):55–70. Also of great value are Robert W. Dent, "Imagination in *A Midsummer Night's Dream*," *Shakespeare Quarterly* 15 (1964):115–29, and Elizabeth Sewell, *The Orphic Voice*, (New Haven: Yale University Press, 1961), pp. 139–41. I have commented on the play in chapters 7 and 8 of my *Shakespeare's Romances* (San Marino, Calif.: Henry E. Huntington Library, 1972).

It is written that the shoemaker should meddle with
his yard and the tailor with his last, the fisher with
his pencil and the painter with his nets; but I am
sent to find those persons whose names are here writ,
and can never find what names the writing person
hath here writ.

*(Romeo
and Juliet
I, ii, 39–
44)*

In much the same way Bottom comments on what he takes
to have been his dream:

The eye of man hath not heard, the ear of man hath not seen,
man's hand is not able to taste, his tongue to conceive, nor his
heart to report, what my dream was.

*(A Mid-
summer
Night's
Dream IV,
i, 211–14)*

Another link between the two plays, and a more serious
one, I find in the way in which the action, though it is entangled enough in both plays, has a frame of longing or
expectation. We do not become bored with the entanglements, tragic or comic, if we are made to share with the
characters some yearning for the conclusion. Juliet expresses this at the end of her great aria on night:

>   So tedious is this day
>   As is the night before some festival
>   To an impatient child that hath new robes
>   And may not wear them.

*(III, ii,
28–31)*

The later comedy, as it establishes its primary symbol of the
moon, expresses a more experienced and adult version of a
similar longing. Theseus says, in the first speech of the play,

>   Now, fair Hippolyta, our nuptial hour
>   Draws on apace. Four happy days bring in
>   Another moon; but O, methinks, how slow
>   This old moon [wanes]! She lingers my desires,
>   Like to a step-dame, or a dowager,
>   Long withering out a young man's revenue.

The plays are linked also, and this has often been noticed, by their imagery. The most striking example seems
characteristically, if not specifically, Shakespearean. It is the
image of love as a flash of lightning. Juliet says, in the balcony scene, just as the lovers are exchanging their vows,

                                        Although I joy in thee,
                        I have no joy of this contract to-night,
                        It is too rash, too unadvis'd, too sudden,
(II, ii,   Too like the lightning, which doth cease to be
116–20)   Ere one can say it lightens.

In the first scene of *A Midsummer Night's Dream*, when
Lysander and Hermia are exclaiming against the tyranny of
outside interference in the love between two people, Lysander, who has studied the subject in literature, but until
now not in life, says,

>   Ay me! for aught that I could ever read,
>   Could ever hear by tale or history,
>   The course of true love never did run smooth;

and he and Hermia go on, in a few lines of stichomythia, to
catalogue the interferences. Then he concludes:

>   Or if there were a sympathy in choice,
>   War, death, or sickness did lay siege to it,
>   Making it momentany as a sound,
>   Swift as a shadow, short as any dream,
>   Brief as the lightning in the collied night,
>   That, in a spleen, unfolds both heaven and earth;
>   And ere a man hath power to say "Behold!"
(I, i, 132–   The jaws of darkness do devour it up:
49)   So quick bright things come to confusion.

This lovely passage almost belongs in *Romeo and Juliet*,
not simply because that marvelous last line almost summa-
rizes the tragedy, but because that word "jaws," now so familiar in another context, in *Romeo and Juliet*, as elsewhere
in Shakespeare, usually refers to death or the grave—here
to darkness, which is its poetic equivalent.

There is a connection, then, between *Romeo and Juliet*
and *A Midsummer Night's Dream*, or rather, there are several, and one of the strongest connections is that of the poetry in the plays, the main subject of my concern. I have
discussed elsewhere the way in which Shakespeare uses poetry in this play to create "landscape"—that is, something
the audience is compelled to visualize which is not, like
"setting," on the stage itself. Some critics call it "word-

painting" or, more vaguely "atmosphere," and some, for instance Richard David, think it is overdone:

The effect of these lyrical flights, in the creation of atmosphere however, is here more striking than in the other plays. Oberon's description of the wounding of the little western flower and of the bank where the wild thyme blows help to produce the sense of a fairy night in the wood, as Hippolita's hunting reminiscences paint the heroic dawn in the valley; this is that use of poetry for suggestive, almost hypnotic effect, which is to play such an important part in the mature tragedies, above all in *Macbeth*. But here [that is, in *MND*] the poetry overflows the bounds of its application; Shakespeare goes on poetizing for its own sake, long after the dramatic effect, at which the poetry aimed, is achieved. The poet and dramatist, in fact, are not yet fused into one.[28]

Another critic, the late Alan Downer, reached a somewhat different conclusion in his classic essay "The Life of Our Design": He was, as always, primarily interested in the plays as dramas presented on the stage. "In seeing Shakespeare on the modern stage," he says,

we take immediate pleasure in the story and a secondary pleasure in the characterization. But certain critical writers have suggested that there is a third and more important pleasure—the meaning as interpreted by the interplay of images. Since we are reasonably deaf to spoken poetry, it would seem that this is a pleasure reserved, as the critics suggest, for the study. Aside from the fact that this makes Shakespeare look a little foolish, like a composer who writes a quartet to be performed by a one-armed violinist, is it true? I believe that it is not; that Shakespeare, if he began as two characters, the Poet and the Playwright, managed to unite them somehow as the Poetic Dramatist; if he began by using the language of action *and* the language of poetry, he soon learned to use the language of *imagery in action* which is the major characteristic of poetic drama.[29]

I welcome Downer's conclusion, naturally, but it saddens me to have him write that "we are reasonably deaf to spoken

28. *The Janus of Poets* (Cambridge: Cambridge University Press, 1935), p. 32.
29. "The Life of Our Design," reprinted in *Modern Shakespearean Criticism*, ed. Alvin B. Kernan (New York: Harcourt, Brace, 1970), p. 33.

poetry." Why should we be? Have we managed to grow tin ears since the last decade of the sixteenth century? I hope the answer is no, but perhaps I should not wait for it.

Let me suggest that there may be a reason why the poetry sticks out, or seems more prominent, in *A Midsummer Night's Dream*. It is, of course, partly a matter of "landscape" or atmosphere—the wood over which Titania and Oberon preside at night and in which Duke Theseus hunts by day is not as familiar to an Elizabethan audience as the court and castle of *Richard II* or the brawling streets and sequestered Friar's cell of an Italian city. But it is also a matter of genre. I said that everybody in *Richard II* is a poet, and I do not wish to retract that. But essentially the play deals with the downfall of a king who was rich in feeling but poor in administrative skills. Much of the poetry in his play derives from this—it is elegiac. *Romeo and Juliet* is a duet in which the characters clothe each other with poetry as their essential means of making love. It is panegyric poetry; of course, in clothing each other they also clothe themselves. Their environment is dark, but they are the streaks of lightning, and then the stars.

A Midsummer Night's Dream is a comedy, and a comedy must have complications. This one is of the simplest; it is the "cross-eyed Cupid" situation which can be resolved only by some trick like the magic juice of some exotic plant. There is not much room—some, but not much—for expression of deep feeling about a single character, as in *Richard*, or about the two central ones, in Verona. Comedy requires detachment. I am struck by Robert Y. Turner's explanation:

By count, *Hamlet* contains more characters with specific names than does *Dream*, and this count includes Peaseblossom, Cobweb, Moth, and Mustardseed, who appear only momentarily to indulge Bottom's whims. The difference lies in the kind of attention given to the characters rather than in the number. In comedy the group seems larger because our attention shifts focus so rapidly from one character to another, a fact which helps preserve the audience's distance from predicaments and encourages laughter. It would be harder, for instance, to become involved with Romeo and Juliet if we were also concerned about the problems of a second pair of lovers; say Benvolio falls in love with Rosaline at the Capulet ball and woos her intermittently throughout the play.[30]

So what shall we say that the poetry in *A Midsummer Night's Dream* does? If the entanglements provide the detachment which is necessary to arouse laughter and hence make the play, in the most fundamental sense, a comedy, the poetry involves our feelings of sympathy and delight and makes it *Shakespearean* comedy. When Peter Quince, Bottom and the rest of them require moonlight for their play they first think of looking in the almanac to see if the moon shines that night, taking practical advantage of a natural phenomenon, and then they fall back on the old habits of the morality plays and have an actor to represent moon. When Shakespeare has need of moonlight to provide an atmosphere for love, he does neither of these. He "reaches back," as they say of a pitcher in baseball, and hurls poetry at us. Possibly the most striking example of his method is not in *A Midsummer Night's Dream* but in the opening of the fifth act of *The Merchant of Venice*. The trial scene in act IV is almost melodrama, and the short scene following it is concerned only with the practical joke the two women play on their husbands about the rings. That perhaps provides some detachment after the haunting exit of Shylock:

> I pray you give me leave to go from hence,
> I am not well. Send the deed after me,
> And I will sign it.

I call it "haunting" not only because anybody who didn't have a heart of stone, like Gratiano, would have a touch of sympathy for Shylock, but I call it "haunting" because of the language. Out of the twenty-four words in those three lines, all but one are monosyllables, and that one exception is the word "after." The bit about the rings is of course a merry jest, a trick played for fun. It dissolves whatever feelings of pathos we have. But what takes their place? Lorenzo and Jessica's catalogue of famous lovers:

30. *Shakespeare's Apprenticeship*, p. 164.

> *Lor:* The moon shines bright. In such a night as this,
> When the sweet wind did gently kiss the trees,
> And they did make no noise, in such a night
> Troilus methinks mounted the Troyan walls,
> And sigh'd his soul toward the Grecian tents
> Where Cressid lay that night.
> *Jes:*   In such a night
> Did Thisby fearfully o'erstrip the dew,
> And saw the lion's shadow ere himself,
> And ran dismayed away.

What was ridiculous when performed by Bottom and his fellows and laughed at by Theseus and his court has been brought unobtrusively back into the realm of moonlight, love, and poetry.

The Merchant of Venice was written not long after *A Midsummer Night's Dream*, I suppose. And if my conjecture that *Richard II*, *Romeo and Juliet*, and *A Midsummer Night's Dream* follow each other in order, the *Merchant* has its proper place right after the lyrical group. At the outset I mentioned that on the poetic side it seems clear that *Richard II* is a successful attempt to "overgo" or surpass Marlowe's *Edward II*. The conclusion that *The Merchant of Venice* is a successful attempt to overgo Marlowe's *Jew of Malta* is neither new nor inherently improbable. Shakespeare knew Marlowe's poetry and apparently loved it, for he had some of it by heart. When, in a pastoral context in *As You Like It*, Phebe suddenly falls in love with Rosalind, whom she takes to be a handsome youth, she says,

> Dead shepherd, now I find thy saw of might,
> "Who ever lov'd that lov'd not at first sight?"

She is quoting *Hero and Leander*, and Marlowe, dead in a tavern brawl, is a shepherd because he composed the most popular lyric for a century to come, "The Passionate Shepherd to His Love."

I have surveyed the three plays sometimes called "The Lyrical Group" without any thesis to argue or prove, merely to call attention to something which puzzles or embarrasses producers and actors and which does not often command the interest of critics because they have other matters in mind—dramatic construction or intellectual background or something else. One must finally stop, and herein will I imitate the Porter in *Macbeth*, a subject which I understand Harry Levin illuminated in this series last year. The Porter describes to the audience, as they sit hearing the knocking at the gate, what types one would find in hell if he were the porter there. He apologizes when he stops to open the gate, because he had many more types to satirize, but the knocking is insistent. So he says, as he opens the gate, "I pray you, remember the porter." I will conclude by saying, "I pray you, remember the poetry."

5 Shakespeare's Variations on Farcical Style

ROBERT B. HEILMAN

I

Let us begin with Coleridge. Much as we refer to his criticism of Shakespeare, we do not often, I believe, recall that he praised *The Comedy of Errors* as an ultimate achievement of its kind: "a legitimate farce in exactest consonance with the philosophical principles of farce, as distinguished from comedy and entertainments."[1] Nor, I suppose, do many people remember Arthur Quiller-Couch's contemptuous reply to Coleridge, issued with the presumptive approval of John Dover Wilson: ". . . farce and comedy have never been and never can be divided into compartments with separate literary laws." Anyway, he went on, "what does it matter?"[2] Though I am anything but a reckless challenger of authority, I believe that all of these old parties are wrong. In my view, *The Comedy of Errors* cannot adequately be described as an ultimate in farce because it is various other things too, and the forms of farce and comedy can indeed be distinguished. By way of prologue I will look at some possible modes of relationship between the distinguishable forms of farce and comedy.

Would the image of the family tree do it? In part, yes. Farce would be the roots—the feeders, the unchanging me-

1. S. T. Coleridge, *Lectures and Notes on Shakespeare and Other Dramatists*, The World's Classics (London: Oxford University Press, 1931), p. 120.
2. In Quiller-Couch's 1922 Introduction, left unchanged by John Dover Wilson in the 2d ed. of *The Comedy of Errors* (Cambridge: Cambridge University Press, 1968), p. xxiii.

chanical system; the full-blown comic forms would be what
we see above ground, with all its enticing variety. But then
the fatal difficulty appears. Comedy can and does occasionally reach a stage at which it does not rely at all on farcical
effects. Unfortunately no tree ever can do without roots.

How about the image of evolution? In this image farce is
the more primitive form—the simpler organism biologi-
cally, or the neolithic man anthropologically. Up to a point
this works nicely enough; it describes, for instance, the development in English drama from the farce of the miracle
plays and earlier sixteenth-century drama to Shakespearean
comedy. But then there is this problem: the more primitive
forms simply don't die out as more primitive forms ought to
do when they have been superseded by more complex
forms. In fact, cultural history may contradict generic evolution by producing what looks like a downhill movement:
i.e., from the Restoration comedy to the more didactic and
sensibilitarian modes of the eighteenth century, and from
these to the less inspired formula theater of the nineteenth
century.

Such facts would seem to drive us to another image,
sometimes called the "myth of nature" and sometimes the
cyclical theory of history. Such a picture of growth, maturity, and decline might be useful for cultural history. But two
problems arise: historical sequences are not my aim, and the
concept of decline is ambiguous. We cannot out of hand
equate decline with a historical succession in which writers
of comedy are followed by writers of farce. To say that Ben
Travers and Alan Ayckbourn are not Wilde and Shaw and
Synge is not to dispose of the later men as decadent left-
overs of a great tradition. That they dominate a theater
which produces no Shaw or Synge may tell us something
about the times. But it tells us nothing about the art practiced by these successors. Their chosen form is farce, and
they use its conventions brilliantly. It appears, then, that we
cannot treat farce as an early stage in evolution or as a late
stage in cyclical decline. It neither fades away into the mists
as a true primitive ought to do, nor finally, as moribund
comedy, sinks into a grave. It is neither the foetus nor the
corpse of comedy. It has a vitality of its own, and hence a

permanent existence on the stage from early times to the
present.

Still, there is a way in which we can use the image of
evolution. We can let it figure not a development in time but
a complicating of structure. In this sense "evolution" de-
notes a logical or schematic relationship: not a temporal before and after, but a formally simpler and more complex.
Comedy does not succeed farce historically but can be developed from it at any time by the addition of new materials
to a basic structure. Farce is not chronologically prior, but
aesthetically more elementary. What we see as the limitations of farce, then, are not so much shortcomings or fail-
ures as they are the defining features of the form and its
primary means of securing the pleasures natural to the form.
By temperament or choice one dramatist sticks to the components of farce and exploits them as best he can, and another adds components that by definition lie outside the
boundaries of farce. By such supplements he is an agent in
this formal evolution of farce into comedy, or, for that matter, into other forms such as romance or melodrama. We can
think of the more complex forms as farce plus altering ingredients.

This metamorphosis by increments, which I call logical
or formal evolution, happens in Shakespeare to be a temporal development from earlier to later. Logical and chronological evolution generally coincide, with some variations
and a deviation for *Merry Wives* in 1600. This is a well-
known history, and there is no need to rehash it. Rather I
want to seek out the concrete elements that make farce
farce, and the elements that change it into something else.
In this quest, time is not of the essence.

II

Farce depends on actions of the body, not of the mind,
soul, or imagination.[3] Like professional wrestling, it is
gymnastics plus stereotyped relationships among the par-

3. Some of the materials in section II, used in a different context and
to a different end, appear in "Farce Transformed: Plautus, Shakespeare,
and Unamuno," *Comparative Literature* 31 (1979): 113–23.

ticipants. Characters run, stumble, fall, duck, trip up others; they are clever or tricky or look stupid or gauche, and in either case the actors must be energetic and agile. Unless exhaustion is a part of the game, the main trait shown is indefatigability. This is possible because no vital strength goes into real thinking, feeling, moral concern, or deliberate choosing and planning. In their stead we get irrationality or absurd reasoning, emotional uproars in popular formulas, noisy assertions of moral indignation, and accidents—especially coincidences—in which fantastically unexpected things, helpful or disruptive, happen to people and speed them on in merry-go-round pursuits and flights like so many wound-up toys. We can then define farce thus: it chooses to depict men and women as essentially mechanical beings without the burdens of mind, feeling, conscience, and will. Of course this platonic idea of farce is not often imitated faultlessly in theatrical practice, which tends to let some touch of mind, feeling, conscience, or will be active in some characters. Will is the element most likely to break in; hence the sudden new schemes, the crazy shifts in direction, and the zany extemporizations that give an air of the voluntary and the novel to the patterns of confusion, rush, and squabble. It is the same in plain farce and its city cousin, bedroom farce. We should be clear that bedroom farce is not porn. In farce, hopeful adulterers itch lightly rather than feel strongly, try rather than succeed, and hurry rather than linger, with maybe a quick flick of skin. But porn offers driving intensity, total success, the interminable osculatory wrestle, and skin by the acre. It is sentimentalism in blue, and always the same; porn corn. In farce this hot-cereal sex, this porn-meal mush, is dehydrated into crisp, crackling nuggets of action to start the play right or keep it moving.

Since our subject is farce in Shakespeare, it is wonderfully convenient that Plautus' *Menaechmi*, the source of *The Comedy of Errors*, is pure farce. The mistaken-identity problem natural to farce lies in the central characters: twin brothers both named Menaechmus, though separated in babyhood and brought up in different towns, Syracuse and Epidamnus, are indistinguishable to everybody. The Syracuse boy, hunting his lost twin for six years, comes to Epidamnus. Surrounded by total strangers, he is called "Menaechmus" by everyone. The last thought to enter his head, however, is that he has found his twin. Such minimal rationality is excluded by convention. Hence continuous mix-ups, squabbles, and quarrels, but no one really feels hurt. Genuine feelings are excluded by convention. The local-boy Menaechmus is carrying on with a fancy woman, for whom he steals jewels and a dress from his wife; in turn the out-of-town Menaechmus steals these from the girl. For either thief, the only problem is to avoid getting caught, or to lie successfully. Any sense of right and wrong is excluded by convention. And then the wrong people keep running into each other; situations are largely brought about by accidents rather than by plan. The will is excluded, though not totally eliminated, by convention. These aspects of the *Menaechmi* clue us in to another fundamental characteristic of farce: its fast pace. This is a secondary quality made mandatory by primary qualities: when there is little or no action of mind, feelings, conscience, or will, there is no depth of character to demand gradual exploration, and movement has to be as fast as possible. For the most part it has to be automatic too. Hence the chase is a standard action in farce.

Thus Plautus does provide us with virtually a Platonic ideal of farce. What does Shakespeare do with it in *The Comedy of Errors*? Actually he proceeds in two totally different ways, and thus we learn some important things about him and his art. His first rule is that if the confusion resulting from coincidence, obtuseness, and automatism is great fun, twice as much confusion will be twice as much fun. So he adds a second pair of twins, each one named Dromio and a slave to one of the original twins, each one now called Antipholus. This doubling virtually quadruples the available confusion, since everybody else has two sets of twins to mix up, and each of four twins can get two other people all mixed up. Hence more numerous arguments and brawls; against only one physical beating in Plautus, Shakespeare has five, with still others planned or announced. In Plautus the stage properties that lead to mix-ups and blows are three; Shakespeare ups them to five. To increase the fun, Shakespeare not only multiplies; he adds too. He tosses in, on the house as it were, the gross kitchen wench who makes a futile sexual pursuit of an unreceptive Dromio, and he greatly expands the realm of verbal farce; while he uses the punning and the three-liner jokes (lead-line, feed-line, and punch-line) that Plautus likes, he also goes in for bigger game, as in the description of Dromio's amorous tormentor by an extended, and often naughty, geographical metaphor.

In effect Shakespeare says to Plautus, "Whatever you can do, I can do twice as much of it." In this, Shakespeare reveals a genuine farcical sensibility, which he lets fly merrily. But at the same time he gives rein to another sensibility which produces, as we know, another kind of theater. For instance, he innovates by putting his Plautine materials in a surprising framework—that of romantic melodrama (such as Plautus does use in other plays, though rather as a convention of entertainment than as a representation of troublesome reality). Aegeon, the father of the twins, hunting a lost son, appears on the same hunting ground, now called Ephesus, where some law makes him eligible for execution. He is in real danger, and we are beyond farce. Further, Aegeon presents his case with dignity and actual pathos, and the Duke of Ephesus, who must judge him, really wavers between legal duty and human pity. This court scene of act I is resumed in act V, when various characters, nearly driven mad by the epidemic confusions, call earnestly for justice. They are given real feelings and some good sense: they are in an orbit outside that of pure farce. And so periodically the play escapes the farcical orbit. Adriana, wife of the home Antipholus, and her sister Luciana have ideas: they argue thoughtfully about the subordination of wives to husbands (II, i), and Adriana, who believes she is wronged, goes beyond the comic-sheet rants of her Plautine predecessor to register genuine feeling. It is farcical when she berates a husband who is the wrong twin, but at the same time she utters a very sober reproach that ends in a paradox: the paradox is that because he is licentious she herself is "possessed with an adulterous blot" since "we two be one" (II, ii, 110–45).[4] This is a metaphysical conceit (it is contemporary with early Donne), that is, an imaginative union of

4. Quotations are from *The Complete Plays and Poems of William Shakespeare*, ed. William Allan Neilson and Charles Jarvis Hill (Boston, Mass.: Houghton Mifflin, 1942).

the thought and feeling which by definition are outside the range of farce. Likewise the immediately following lockout scene, based on Plautus' *Amphitruo*, is mainly farce: the local Antipholus, shut out of his house while the visiting Antipholus is dining inside with Adriana and Luciana, rages around, trades abuse with servants, and wants to break down the door. But then Shakespeare suddenly moves away from farce when Balthazar urges the furious husband to have "patience," to guard his "reputation," to recall the "honour" of his wife and his long experience of her "wisdom,/ . . . virtue, . . . and modesty," and to wait for a later explanation instead of increasing an uproar that will arouse "vulgar comment" (III, i). Patience and reasonableness and decorum belong to a full humanity that lies outside the boundaries of farce, as does Antipholus' partial acceptance of sensible advice. Again, when Luciana lectures the wrong Antipholus for supposed infidelity to his wife Adriana, she neither rages nor flirts but quietly urges upon him the worldly good form often espoused in comedy: if you must err, be decorous, not blatant. The alien Antipholus falls in love with Luciana, and we have another tone, that of romantic comedy rather than of farce. The aggrieved wife Adriana may at times fall into farcical rant, but she can also assert, "Ah but I think him better than I say," and "my heart prays for him, though my tongue do curse" (IV, ii), she can be truly concerned when he is arrested, and she can be trapped by the Abbess' clever interrogation into acknowledging herself a nagging wife. Here is some genuine comedy of character, and it enriches the batch of act V settlements that end the play mainly on a romantic note.

We might deal with the diversity of the play either by blaming Shakespeare for mixing up apparently discordant ingredients, or by praising him for not being content with the farcical. But rather than praising or blaming, I want only to emphasize the co-presence of two different artistic sensibilities and the way in which each one produces its own kind of pleasurable effects. Shakespeare gives no sign of being apologetic about the farcical sensibility—the interest in a primitive humanity—and he never wholly denies it, though, as he goes on to other plays, he either gives it a more peripheral role or very ingeniously transforms it by portrayals of men who have evolved further on the scale of human possibility.

The Taming of the Shrew contains much farce, but it has significant evolutionary tendencies. There is traditional farce of confused identity in the Lucentio-loves-Bianca plot, but with two changes from *The Comedy of Errors*: we have nothing so mechanical as indistinguishable twins, for the confusions result from assumed identities—that is, from acts of the will, which, as I have said, is usually the first addition to the skeleton personality of farce. Again, in the Prologue, Sly is the drunken man who is a staple of farce in all times: all that is left of character is a physical lower-common-denominator. The trick played upon Sly is the practical joke which is another staple of farce: the scheming will is there but none of the sensitivity that would make the trick hurtful. The practical joke is an extension of slapstick: of the blows, either physical or verbal, that are noisy but innocuous. There is much of this effect when Kate and Petruchio are making their frenetic scenes.

But beneath all this characteristic uproar and hullabaloo is the farcical heart of the matter, the translation of farce into psychological terms. The idea of the taming is purely farcical. Farcical in what sense? In the sense that the remaking of a human being is imaged as the training of an animal and that this training is based wholly on the belief in automatic responses to stimuli. Automatic responses are the inevitable style in a realm where thought, feeling, and conscience are not yet the central determinants of action. Thus we see automatism everywhere in farce: everybody is automatically hungry or thirsty or libidinous, automatically suspicious or jealous, defensive or scheming, automatically responsive to carrot and stick. But when, as in the taming, automatic responses lead to a change in personality, we have what we might call farce in depth.

Yet the irony of it is that what evolves from the farcical conception is, amazingly, a comedy of character. We see animal trainer and trainee, not as man with a whip and broken woman, but as two good human beings. Within the tamer there is the loving man; there is no doubt of his fond-

ness, and of his decent and civilized nature. And while Kate
is technically submissive, we do not sense her as beaten into
a lifeless automaton; rather she is freed from a curse and
delivered, by discovery of a better self, into a better, freer,
more imaginative life. Ironically, a farcical conception
evolves into a comic situation—that is, one based on a
genuine humanity of feeling and intelligence. This transformation into comedy is the clearer if we compare it with
Charles Marowitz's *The Shrew*, which converts farce into
bitter satire: Marowitz sees only a sadistic trainer and a cruel
seductive shrew, with a female victim in chains and a male
victim in matrimonial slavery to a tyrant-bitch. Petruchio
beats up Kate, chains her, and rapes her; while Bianca, by
an alternation of weeping, screaming, and erotic tantalizing, brings Lucentio to the altar not only tamed but broken.

III

So much for two plays in which farce is unmistakably
primary but in which we can also observe clear evolutionary
movements. Shakespeare uses farcical materials in many
other plays. With passing time, as we know, it has a lesser
role, but it may provide a significant functional accent. *Two
Gentlemen of Verona* and *Love's Labor's Lost* have a somewhat special cast in that they show Shakespeare taking a
good deal of pleasure in what may be called "verbal farce."
I allude, of course, to the rapid-fire word-play that is sometimes witty but frequently has an air of mechanical routines,
as in the patter of stand-up comedians. Stichomythic exchanges—in less scholarly argot, one-liners—suggest a
pop-gun rat-a-tat-tat rather than the fencing of true minds.
Furthermore, *The Two Gentlemen* frequently relies on a kind
of deliberate malapropism or laborious punning. And when
Launce the servant soliloquizes on the ill-timed and mis-
placed urinations, and so forth, of his dog, we are in the
elementary physical life of the farcical world.

But these are somewhat superficial aspects of the play.
More important is that in *Two Gentlemen*, the main actions
have an automatic quality that makes them implicitly farcical. Now it may seem very strange to apply the word *farci-*

cal to the rivalry of two lovers, a betrayal, an attempted
rape, parental pressure on lovers, banishment, midnight escapes, noble outlaws, and so on. These are among the
stereotypes of romance. Yet they do not come off well; they
are unconvincing. The difficulty, I suggest, is this: Shakespeare is using romantic materials but does not yet have a
feeling for them and is unconsciously thinking and working
farcically—i.e., devising sudden effects and actional sleights-
of-hand rather than creating plausible romantic emotion. He
isn't getting into his characters; they are little more than
automats in stereotyped actions. Proteus is *in* and *for* love;
Valentine is neither. Valentine suddenly falls in love, whereupon Proteus promptly forgets his own true love and falls in
love with Valentine's girl Silvia. Proteus betrays Valentine;
Valentine is instantly banished and instantly made a head of
a band of noble outlaws. Thus he is right there for a rescue
when Proteus endeavors to rape Silvia in the forest. Quick
as a wink the foiled rapist, Proteus, in just five lines (V, iv,
73–77) repents of all his evil deeds. Swept away by the
flashflood of new moral delicacy, Valentine, in just seven
lines, not only forgives Proteus but gives up to him "All
that was mine in Silvia" (V, iv, 77–83). We are doubtless
supposed to admire true brotherhood, but it is hard to forget
Silvia. Poor girl, she is allowed no lines at all to say how
she feels about this instant nobility that gives her away like
an unusable present generously passed on to someone else
every December 25.

   Now such actions, though romantic in superficial color-
ing, are really farcical in nature. They are sudden moves
and surprises, essentially outside character. The fast pace
and kaleidoscopic shifts substitute for the depth that requires a gradual development of character and prevents a
high-speed rush into novelties. The trouble, of course, is
that at spots in *Two Gentlemen* Shakespeare attributes just
enough non-routine feeling to the participants to prevent a
wholly farcical effect. We are supposed to censure Proteus'
infidelity and admire his penitence, whereas we hardly believe in either and would probably relish them more if they
were done in a Groucho Marx style. We are caught between
the approval and disapproval demanded by romance and

the voluntary suspension of both approval and disapproval demanded by farce. Shakespeare is wandering between two worlds, one far from dead and the other only half born.

In *Love's Labor's Lost* the famous word-games create a more complex verbal drama than that of the *Two Gentlemen of Verona*. Along with the verbal farce there are playful parodies of fashionable styles—sonnets and euphuism and scholarship—and dexterous jests which are not automatic comebacks but reflect a critical taste and intelligence. Thus to the minimal personality of farce has been added, among other things, some mental activity. Just as the language moves away from pure farcicality, so does the action. A real play of ideas hangs over the plot: the idea that men may value study enough to try to pursue it to an impossible ascetic extreme, the idea that such discipline needs to be complemented by human love, and, most important, the idea that love-at-first-sight, love though it seem, may not be a wholly reliable guide to life. Further, in the succession of these ideas we can see Shakespeare using his plot in a remarkable way. He makes it in effect a critique of the farcical type of action which in earlier plays he has relied upon heavily. His four young men act repeatedly as if life could have a farcical pace: they *rush* headlong into a monastic triennium of loveless study, then they rush out of it and headlong into study-less love, and indeed they try to rush their four darlings into instant responses, as automatic as in farce (the four parallel cases of course resemble the mechanical action of farce). These high-speed actions do not wholly by-pass human nature, as farce ideally does, but they utilize only a small part of it; the men's impulsive moves are like farcical improvization.

But *Love's Labor's Lost* improves greatly on *The Two Gentlemen of Verona* because now the hurried actions are regularly subject to criticism by elements of the drama. Biron (Berowne), though he goes along with the monastic study program, questions it in a way that farce would never think of. Still more effective than that, however, is the female quartet's criticism of the scholars' equally hasty turn from scholarship to love. The women do not automatically think the haste inevitable or enchanting, as girls in farce would do; rather they see that it may reveal fickleness of being instead of durable emotion. The young men need questioning, taking down, testing. So the ladies, exhibiting both will and judgment, impose a one-year delay and a series of disciplinary tasks which can prove the genuineness of the male feeling; thus the mechanisms of farce give way to a moral probation which is wholly non-farcical. What is more, the tasks assigned by the ladies faintly suggest the men's recent monastic life; thus the moral probation implicitly asserts that there was something valuable in the original scholarly program—that program into which, and then out of which, the young men had dashed like robots. Man can ludicrously overdo the ascetic, but asceticism means a discipline that has value. Here, then, there are marked additions to a farcical base—will and feeling and ideas that include a critique of the farcical.

At *first* glance *A Midsummer Night's Dream* may seem to have moved outside the arena of farce. Then at second glance one may say, "But no—there's the 'lamentable comedy' and 'tragical mirth' of Quince and company's 'Pyramus and Thisby' (I, ii, 11–13; V, i, 57). Surely *it* is farcical." I suggest that it is not really so. In the inset play, people are actively planning; they are not predictable automats but individuals endeavoring, with imagination and a strong desire to please, to produce good theater. What causes our laughter is not a rush-hour thinness of personality but a naïve, good-humored defect of talent. Their stagework produces not the farce of fast-paced confusion but the traditional comedy of an incongruity between self-image and the facts of life. Yet *A Midsummer Night's Dream*, though in the main it evokes fairyland, enchanted forest, moonlit misty midnight, and all the charms of lunatic, lover, and poet, still has some of its major roots deep in the soil of farce. The mixed-up love pairings in acts II and III are, I suggest, what we might find in a master farceur like Georges Feydeau or Alan Ayckbourn. The cause of the mismatings is outside human choice: it is the eye-drops that stir up maddeningly scrambled passions. Likewise there is coincidence: people always happen to be where, when medicated eyes open, they fall upon the person whose being seen will create trouble. Again, pure mistake is basic: Puck, the eye-doctor, gets the wrong patient, Lysander instead of Demetrius, and the situation is worse than it was before. All is coincidental, external; even Demetrius' final return to Helena is due to eye-drops rather than change of heart. The eye-crossed lovers snap at each other and the men prepare to fight—exactly the quick farcical bellicosity, and of course with a farcical rejection of the depth that could cause disaster. The verbal exchanges are often in the rapid-fire stichomythic style. There is an artificial symmetry as in farce: the two men first pursue Hermia, and then both pursue Helena—a kind of miniature chase in which everyone runs madly in one direction and then equally madly in the other. Finally there is the practical joke that is so frequent in farce when the will starts operating: Oberon uses eye-drops on Titania and thus makes her fall in love with Bottom, who has been turned into an ass, at least from the neck up. Thus Titania, as if hypnotized rather than making a decision, does as Oberon wants.

But we must not overstate the farcical. Above all the mistakes and coincidences lies the magic of the fairies; the natural tools of farce are in the hands of a power outside of nature. Thus we have a new dimension, and at the risk of sounding a bit fancy, we might call it metaphysical farce. Mistakes, jests, and good deeds, though they do not represent human choice, still are the work of a superhuman agency. The intervention of cosmic powers confers on human beings a dignity not present when they are merely the creatures of mischance, automatic responses, and faulty headwork. And the characters themselves are capable of dignity; for the most part, Helena registers the real pain of desertion and then the indignation of one who thinks she is the butt of two sham lovers. Once harmony is restored, all lovers reflect on the preceding mix-ups in a thoughtful way not admissible in pure farce. And even the amatory mix-ups do not exist entirely for confusion's sake: in a way they embody an idea. They are a commentary on the waywardness and unpredictability of human passion. Eye-dropper Puck is a new incarnation of blind Cupid. In sum, Shakespeare here makes enthusiastic use of various routines of farce. In no way does he disdain the kinds of entertainment that these routines afford, but he partly transforms farce by the play of ideas, the presence of feeling, and the participation of powers whose presence and concern enlarge the human stature of partly farcical beings. What takes place is another little movement of evolution.

Though one could go on through all the other comedies and trace variations on and evolutions from farce, the assembled evidence might be more extensive than profitable (in *Merry Wives*, for instance, the practical-joke version of farce is little tempered by more spacious concerns). So I shall skip some plays entirely and with others rely more on quick assertion than extended demonstration. In *Much Ado About Nothing* the literal farcical matters (Borachio's drunkenness and the verbal farce in the longwinded dialogue of those improbable constables Dogberry and Verges) are, as in *The Taming*, less interesting than the psychological farce at the heart of the Benedick-Beatrice relationship. There is much of the automatic in these two—in their initial skepticism of love and, more importantly of course, in the susceptibility of each of them to the report that he is loved by the other. And this automatic responsiveness is stimulated by the external action of matchmakers, who are carrying out what we might call the benevolent practical joke (the eyedrop treatment translated into friendly whispers). Just as Kate is saved from shrewishness by action from without, so Benedick and Beatrice are saved from each other by action from without. But in *Much Ado* the enrichment of basic farce by the materials of genuine personality is carried much further: here we have the beneficial interaction of two people rather than the therapeutic moulding of one by the other; both undergo modification; and both exhibit their full humanity in a larger testing experience outside their own relationship.

There is a special kind of interest in two groups of plays—those usually called "dark comedies" and those usually called "dramatic romances"—for neither type seems a likely host to farce. In these plays we do not find an evolution from farce; rather, plays that are very serious make surprising brief dips into the old bag of farcical materials and methods. The farcical becomes, if not a strong presence, at least a sturdy accent. *Measure for Measure* is an intense melodrama, for only an extraordinary rescue prevents a triumph of genuine evil. Yet here we find a stupid, misspeaking, longwinded constable, a reincarnation of Dogberry and Verges in *Much Ado*. Much of what he does and says is entertainment for its own sake. Yet at the same time all this is a minor parallel to the central problem in the major plot: the executors of justice, at both levels, are less than ideally equipped for their tasks. Like the tail of a kite, the farce is functional. Pompey the pimp and Mistress Overdone the brothel-keeper are partly farcical in make-up—she with her nine husbands, and he in his obfuscation of a legal hearing (II, i, 85 ff.). But in a more underlying way they represent a kind of farcical concept: sex as an ongoing automatic activity. Everyone remembers Pompey's famous comment on sexual reform in Vienna: "Does your worship mean to geld and splay all the youth in the city . . . they will to't then" (II, i, 226 ff.). Now that is exactly the principle of bedroom farce, and its presence here is a rather lighthearted reminder of the urgent human mechanisms that reformers must deal with or live with. The farce echoes functionally the very serious issue in the behavior of Angelo, the Duke's deputy who turns into a ruthless bedroom schemer. Yet the play as a whole differs from bedroom farce, since such farce admits neither consequences nor penalties. *Measure for Measure*, however, reminds us of unwanted pregnancies, diseases, and imprisonment. Hence the farcical interpolations in a moral melodrama steadily carry a realistic value that farce itself excludes.

Likewise in the late romances Shakespeare introduces some materials of farcical nature or potentiality but then lets them evolve into another kind of thing. In *Cymbeline* the oafish Cloten could be, and in an earlier play might have been, simply a figure of farcical brainlessness. But his vanity is satirized; in pursuing Imogen he becomes a vengeful plotter; and he even has a touch of the English patriot—all developments away from farce. Then there is the great moment when Imogen discovers Cloten's beheaded body dressed in her husband's clothes. Imogen not only takes the

body to be her husband's but spells out the physical characteristics of the body which she is sure she recognizes.
This is surely a late, and very subtle, revision of the identity
farce of the early plays—and farce daringly introduced at a
moment of apparent disaster.

Finally in *The Tempest* Shakespeare takes a perennial
farcical subject, drunkenness, and gives it his fullest treatment in Trinculo and Stephano. For the most part they are
laughably out of control, or improbably plotting, or foolishly stealing: all farce. Shakespeare innovates strikingly
when he has savage Caliban mistake the drunken pair for
divinities: here we get a farcical version of religious worship. Yet, as in *Measure for Measure*, Shakespeare has
given his farce a functional role: the devout Caliban leads
his gods into a revengeful, power-seizing plot against Prospero. It cannot succeed. Yet in this abortive snatch at control
of the island we have a farcical parallel to the mainland
usurpation of which Prospero has been a real victim. This
provides a remarkable treatment of the power-grabbing
theme in two different keys. Here, too, we have a touch of
what I called metaphysical farce as in *A Midsummer Night's
Dream*: Puck is now Ariel, playing supernatural practical
jokes, all beneficent, helping to right old wrongs and prevent a new one. And Ariel's leading the trio of would-be
revolutionaries, two still drunk, on a wild-goose chase
through nettles and thorns and into a filthy pool is exactly
analogous to that great Elizabethan practical joke of tricking
or tossing a victim into the jakes.

IV

So much for this very hasty sketch of the persistence of
the farcical in Shakespeare's comedies, and its use even in
those where one might least expect it. One might moralize
this tale in different ways. It would of course take a pretty
puritanical critic to regret the presence of farce in contexts
of threatened disaster, of thoughtfulness, of the poetic reordering of reality. It would be much too easy, on the other
hand, to assert that Shakespeare progressively moves away
from farce, and that this movement coincides with his grad-

ual mastery of more advanced comic forms. That would simply be offering new evidence for what no one is disposed to doubt. Hence, as I said earlier, I do not regard blame and praise as suitable activities in this context. In tracing Shake-spearian farce my aim is not to denigrate or glorify, but to characterize a certain kind of artistic procedure. While it has been helpful to use the image of generic evolution to clarify the relationship between farce and comic or other forms, the more urgent problem is to escape from a loose use of the term *farce* and to try to identify a neutral, objective content for the word. This means resisting two attitudes to farce which do not define it impartially. The older attitude, of course, treats farce as an *inferior* thing that adult minds should ignore, disdain, or apologize for. Then in recent dec-ades there has been the customary pendular swing in the history of ideas, and farce has been puffed up toward a new weight and meaning. For instance, such dramatists as Io-nesco and Dürrenmatt apply the term "tragic farce" to some of their plays. They may, of course, be trying to surprise or be speaking ironically, but I suspect that they are ascribing to farce a depth or range that we have not been aware of. This is exactly what has been done by certain *critics* en-gaged in rehabilitating farce. They see it not only as basic in comedy but as an expression of human rebelliousness, as a carrier of man's resentments against the establishment and the system, indeed as a symptom of the anarchic bent in his personality, and even of a secret longing for chaos. Such theorizing goes too easily and rashly in the opposite direc-tion; one can make a case for farce without magnifying it into a symbolic loophole for the residual anarchist and Ya-hoo and destroyer in man. But it is right to defend farce, for farce remains enjoyable to mature men and women, and they need not apologize for it or on the other hand give the experience a dose of moral growth-hormones and stretch it into a psychic safety-valve job. As technically the presen-tation of man at a level of mechanical, physical existence— i.e., with little, if any, thought, feeling, moral concern, or will—farce has a clear function in the general human scene. It provides a temporary escape from responsibility, a holi-day from both the vulnerability that cannot be eradicated and the obligations that may not be refused, in the actual world. Farce is an hour's respite from order and from the categorical imperative to seek it. It does not enact an unconscious desire to tear down; rather it provides a siesta in the long Atlantean labor of holding up. It offers a brief truancy, in sum, not from external pressures and systems, but from the inescapable burdens of being fully human.

With such a concept of farce, we can free ourselves from the old routine of seeing Shakespeare as going from worse to better or from a lesser to a greater potentiality. Instead we can see him working from different poles in the surveying of human personality and as gratifying his audiences by means of different theatrical methods, opening different realms of aesthetic experience that correspond to different operating styles of our human nature. On the one hand, men and women are creatures of high thought and deep feeling and idealism and at the same time capable of ignoring these or reversing them or corrupting them to their own ends. On the other hand, they are mechanisms who do not see or think or feel much or well, and who instead dash about in confusion, clash easily but undestructively, act by instinct and react by stock response, trick or are tricked (when will comes into play), seek quick satisfactions, are thrown into quick distresses, and in the end are always rescued. Shakespeare can do it both ways, and with many variations between the extremes.

This may or may not be the right case to make for farce as a distinctive method rather than a youthful insufficiency or a later lapse from the heights. Be that as it may, we cannot fail to see that Shakespeare makes remarkably diverse use of the farcical mode. He uses farcical materials as direct entertainment in their own right. He notably combines them with other materials that lead to quite different tones. He uses what I have called a farcical concept of character and yet works out from this base into an expanding personality that becomes fuller than one might expect. He is aware of, and at least one time I think inadvertently falls into, the movements of personality that are implicitly farcical even when the foreground drama asks us to feel more serious human tensions. Overall, then, we find a variegated em-

ployment of farce, from a pleasure in itself to "farcical relief" and, beyond that, on to a somewhat elusive symbol of
the presence, in an adult world where humanity is presumably adequate, of ways of acting and reacting that, if not
actually primitive, are closer to the automatic than one
might expect. This last, if I am not mistaken, appears rather
subtly in the plays called "dark" and those called "romances." Here, where misdeeds closer to active evil than is
usual in comedy are meeting with requital and where sharp
problems of justice are being canvassed, the farcical strands
in the action are reminders of the mechanical life, of the
animal perhaps, that push on not much changed by crisis
and moral reordering. Reform catches the outstanding misdeeds, but still there is something unregenerate that goes on
its way, automatic and unlikely to be modified by the qualities that make for full humanity. In the bedroom farce of
Roman and twentieth-century theater this single-track energetic life always makes ritual obeisances to the oughts and
musts of the community, but at most it is interrupted, not
inhibited, in its merry instinctual steeplechase. In Shakespeare the lowest-common-denominator somatic life belongs to a peripheral minority, and yet one that in its persistence may speak for a considerable slice of human nature
generally. In the last plays the physical-fleshly is much over-
shadowed by the lives that transform the farcical or transcend its limits, but it is not finally eclipsed. It persists here
as the final version, in some ways the most substantial one,
of that primitiveness of being which, in the earlier Shake-
spearian versions of farce, manifests itself in confused
scampering, slapstick, flytings, rapid motion, and quick
stock responses. Shakespeare has seen the connection between many regions in the realm of farce, and between farce
and other realms.

Shakespeare and the Ceremonies of Romance

6

EUGENE M. WAITH

Ceremonial scenes had an understandable appeal for the Tudor playwright. They were occasions for the visual splendor that all forms of pageantry could provide, and, as Alice Venezky pointed out many years ago,[1] they reproduced spectacles already popular in progresses, welcoming pageants, Lord Mayor's shows, and the like. Although pre-Restoration London theaters could not achieve the effects contrived by Inigo Jones for the court masque, we should not underestimate what they were able to do with costume and movement, occasionally assisted by the machinery of trap-doors and suspension gear. But what pleased the public aroused Jonson's scorn and is frequently dismissed by literary critics today as "mere" spectacle. Often it was more than this. We are becoming increasingly aware of the theatrical impact of such ceremonies as the division of the kingdom in *King Lear* or the banquet in *Macbeth*. My subject is certain kinds of ceremonies which occurred in romances and which a playwright could use to support the ideas characteristic of romance.

When the perennially popular romance began to be dramatized in the 1570s, one of its attractions was no doubt the opportunities it offered to render the marvelous in theatrical terms. Two related forms of the marvelous, so typical of romance that they are almost emblematic of it, are the mysterious forces beyond man's control, which help or hinder him, and what is represented as the capacity of some men to transcend the usual human limitations in pursuit of

1. *Pageantry on the Shakespearean Stage* (New York: Twayne, 1951).

an ideal. Of the ceremonies which correspond to these forms of the marvelous I shall comment first on theophanies and certain ceremonies related to divine intervention in human affairs and then on ceremonies of self-transcendence.

The romances that Elizabethan dramatists were putting on the stage were blends of the chivalric romance of the Middle Ages and several other literary forms, including the so-called "Greek romance," with its shipwrecks, pirates, concealed identities, and sorely tried lovers. Fortune and Providence play important parts in these stories, as do the gods, whose plans are often cryptically revealed in oracles. In *The Rare Triumphs of Love and Fortune*, performed before the queen in 1582, and one of the earliest surviving dramatized romances, the seemingly capricious influence of the gods on human life is made the explicit point of the framing action, a quarrel between Venus and Fortune over which of them is more powerful. The story of the lovers in the main action is alternately dominated by one goddess or the other until Jupiter ends their conflict and all is well. The doings of the gods are obviously to be presented in a spectacular fashion. A fury rises at their first appearance to set them quarreling; "shows" of Troilus and Cressida, Alexander, and others are mounted to testify to the power of the rival goddesses; the "triumphs" of Fortune at the end of acts II and IV and of Venus at the end of Act III call for drums and trumpets for one goddess and viols for the other, as processions march about the stage; and in the last act Venus and Fortune "show themselves" in some way to the human characters.[2] Here an abundance of spectacular ceremony demonstrates the awesome difference between human and divine intrigue.

By the end of the first decade of the seventeenth century both the material and the techniques of the early dramatized romances had become old-fashioned if not downright ludicrous, but to a much more sophisticated dramatist the very quaintness may have been tempting. In his last plays Shakespeare seems to have made a deliberate effort to remind his audiences of an outworn mode and at the same time, by

2. See Malone Society Reprints (Oxford: Oxford University Press, 1931), sigs. Aii–Bii, Cii, Div, Fiv–Giv[v].

reviving some of its devices, to achieve new effects. The use of Gower in *Pericles* is an obvious example of archaizing, and in other ways as well the play recalls the mode of romance more precisely than does a romantic comedy like *As You Like It*. In no play of Shakespeare's are the sudden turns of fortune more conspicuous. "Clearly," as F. D. Hoeniger puts it, "the course of Pericles' life is shaped mainly by Providence. . . ."[3] Shakespeare uses certain ceremonial scenes to emphasize this shaping.

Of the play's many ceremonies, including dumb shows, a banquet, and a procession of knights on their way to a tournament, the most impressive are those of the last act which mark the happy reversal of Pericles' ill fortune. A theophany, though very brief, is important: Diana appears to summon Pericles to her altar at Ephesus. This vision immediately succeeds the ceremony of Marina's reunion with her father and leads to the ceremony at Diana's temple, in which Pericles and Thaisa are reunited. Recovery and a kind of rebirth are the import of these moving scenes, and their power is greatly enhanced by their formality. In the first of them, on board ship, Pericles is apparently concealed by a curtain until, at Lysimachus' request, it is drawn back to reveal the king sunk in his speechless torpor. The process of his revival by Marina is stretched over some hundred and fifty lines as she first sings to him and then gradually induces him to talk with her. Much of the dialogue concerns the bits of information which lead to the recognition—her name, the circumstances of her birth, her father's name. The deliberate pacing, the rituals of revealing and then reclothing Pericles when he demands "fresh garments," and the "heavenly music" he hears are all conducive to a sense of strangeness and wonder also expressed in the fine poetry of the culminating portion of the scene. As it is ending Pericles falls asleep, and Diana appears. This supernatural happening is only the most wonderful event in a scene of growing wonder—an appropriate climax to the miraculous restoration of Marina.

The scene at the temple of Diana with its specifically

3. *Pericles*, ed. F. D. Hoeniger (London: Methuen, 1963), p. lxxx. All quotations are from this edition.

religious ceremony follows immediately, completing both
the previous ceremony and the play. The return to Ephesus
recalls the scene in act III in which the chest containing the
body of Thaisa is opened. Here, too, is a ceremony of restoration, as servants bring "napkins and fire," music plays,
and Cerimon brings Thaisa back to life. During the more
elaborate ceremony at the temple, where Pericles, accompanied by Marina and several others, is praying to the goddess, Thaisa, now a priestess, faints as she recognizes her
husband. Reviving her recapitulates again the pattern of loss
and recovery, near-death and rebirth, to which the earlier
ceremonies contributed. Shakespeare seizes upon the wonderful way in which the victims of misfortune are mysteri-
ously rescued and gives it a thematic significance only
hinted at in his source.

The intervention of the gods in human affairs sometimes
recalls the epic tradition of the "descent from heaven," about
which Thomas Greene has written.[4] There a mortal may be
prompted and guided as Priam is at the end of the *Iliad* by
Iris and Hermes, or reminded of his duty as Aeneas is by
Mercury in the *Aeneid*. Diana's appearance in *Pericles* may
reflect this tradition, but a more obvious example is to be
found in *Clyomon and Clamydes*, probably performed in
the late 1570s or early 1580s,[5] a play which contains even
less than *Love and Fortune* to stimulate thought and much
to repel the lover of artistic excellence. The crudity of the
dramatic structure is only less remarkable than the wood-
enness of the verse. The Prologue proclaims the concerns
of chivalric and Greek romance when he tells us that in the
pages of "worthy writers," where "Noble acts and deeds of
many hidden lurks, / Our Author he hath found the Glasse
of glory shining bright," and promises that we shall see lovers buffeted by Fortune, finding both joy and "hugie heapes
of care" (ll. 1–10). The episode of divine intervention occurs toward the end of the play. The Princess Neronis, loved
by Clyomon, has escaped from the clutches of the wicked

4. *The Descent from Heaven* (New Haven: Yale University Press,
1963), p. 99.
5. See *Clyomon and Clamydes*, ed. Betty J. Littleton (The Hague:
Mouton, 1968), pp. 30–33. All quotations are from this edition.

king of Norway and is wandering in the forest, dressed as a shepherd's boy, when she comes upon a "hearse" (that is, a coffin), surmounted by the golden shield of Clyomon. Assuming that her knight is slain, she prays the gods for mercy in a song and prepares to commit suicide. As she is kneeling before the hearse, Providence descends, sent by Jove, and hands her verses which tell her that Clyomon is alive and that the dead body is that of Norway, whom he killed (ll. 1532–73).

Crude as it is, this scene of prayer, preparation for suicide, and divine intervention is genuinely theatrical and makes its point in the obvious and striking way of pageants. When Shakespeare devised the spectacular scene of Posthumus' vision in *Cymbeline* (V, iv) he must have had the tradition of the descent from heaven in mind and possibly this specific scene from *Clyomon and Clamydes*.[6] In some of the verse James Nosworthy believes that he was influenced by speeches of the gods in *Love and Fortune*.[7] That he went far beyond his models comes as no surprise.

Elaborate stage directions permit us to envisage the scene in *Cymbeline* in some detail. Posthumus, overwhelmed with guilt for his mistreatment of Imogen, prays to the gods to take his life as he lies in prison. Then, as he sleeps, "solemn music" plays, after which certain musicians precede the stately entrance of two ghosts—his father, dressed as a warrior, and his mother. After more music his dead brothers appear with the wounds they received in battle. The first stage direction concludes: *"They circle Posthumus round as he lies sleeping"* (V, iv, 29 SD). Next the Leonatus family appeals to Jupiter to intervene on behalf of the unfortunate Posthumus. Another stage direction brings the scene to its climax: *"Jupiter descends in thunder and lightning, sitting upon an eagle: he throws a thunderbolt. The Ghosts fall on their knees"* (l. 92 SD). Even in the public theater, which had nothing like the equipment available at court, this must have been a startling moment, and when the play was per-

6. See Hallett Smith, *Shakespeare's Romances* (San Marino, Calif.: Henry E. Huntington Library, 1972), p. 15.

7. *Cymbeline*, ed. J. M. Nosworthy (London: Methuen, 1955), p. xxxvi. All quotations are from this edition.

formed years later for Charles I and Henrietta Maria, the vision of Posthumus was doubtless done full justice.

After hurling his thunderbolt Jupiter rebukes the Leonati for their complaints, assures them that Posthumus will be reconciled to Imogen, and gives them a tablet to lay on Posthumus' breast. He then ascends and the ghosts vanish. Posthumus awakes, reads the oracular tablet, and is appropriately puzzled. For the audience, more clearly than for him, the descent of Jupiter foreshadows the happy ending brought about by the many recognitions of the last scene.

Ceremonies such as these give force to the dramatic presentation of sudden reversals of fortune and of the idea that the world is "a mighty maze, but not without a plan." G. Wilson Knight has written repeatedly of the intimations of "myth and miracle" in the last plays and has called attention to theophanies such as those in *Pericles* and *Cymbeline*.[8] *The Winter's Tale* has no theophany, but its most famous scene is contrived to *seem* miraculous, and once again the impression is sustained by ceremony. A quasi-religious tone pervades the statue scene, leading some to guess that it takes place in Paulina's private chapel. It is, in any case, a very special place with a curtained niche, apart from the gallery where she displays her other "singularities." In only one other scene of the play is there so religious an atmosphere—in the description of the Delphic Oracle by Cleomenes and Dion:

> I shall report,
> For most it caught me, the celestial habits
> (Methinks I so should term them), and the reverence
> Of the grave wearers. O, the sacrifice!
> How ceremonious, solemn and unearthly
> It was i' th' offering![9]

"Ceremonious, solemn, and unearthly" Paulina makes the unveiling of the supposed statue of Hermione by Julio Romano. "O royal piece!" says Leontes:

---

8. *The Crown of Life* (London: Cumberlege, 1947), p. 192, et passim.
9. *The Winter's Tale*, ed. J. H. P. Pafford (London: Methuen, 1963), III, i, 3–8. All quotations are from this edition.

> There's magic in thy majesty, which has
> My evils conjur'd to remembrance, and
> From thy admiring daughter took the spirits,   *(V, iii,*
> Standing like stone with thee.   *38–42)*

Perdita then falls to her knees to implore a blessing of this quasi saint.

The immediately ensuing dialogue and action comprise the capstone to the much-discussed treatment of the theme of art and nature running through the play. Leontes and Polixenes are astounded at the lifelikeness of the "statue"; Paulina offers to make it move; and then—a moment which can be extraordinarily affecting no matter how often it has been experienced—Hermione steps down from the pedestal. The power of this moment derives not only from its connection with the important theme of art and nature, but also, and perhaps primarily, from the depiction of Leontes' repentance and of his reunion with Hermione. Elements from the scenes of Posthumus' vision and Pericles' reunion with daughter and wife are compressed into a more intense dramatic experience. As in *Pericles*, the ceremony strongly suggests a kind of rebirth. But unlike Pericles, Leontes is directly responsible for the near-tragic separations which are thus ended. Like Posthumus, he already repents of his mistreatment of his wife. Indeed, it is the fantastic premise of this romantic tale that he has repented for sixteen years, while Paulina has kept Hermione on ice, so to speak, and Perdita has had time to grow up. But of this period of his life we know almost nothing. The statue scene dramatizes his feelings, and its contrivance allows for a far more effective portrayal of them than of Posthumus' remorse in his brief prayer before his vision. Leontes is so "transported" by the sight of Hermione that Paulina threatens to draw the curtain again, but Leontes protests that his "affliction has a taste as sweet / As any cordial comfort" (V, iii, 76–77). Paulina then makes the magic she is about to perform conditional upon the awakening of Leontes' faith. Only then, to the accompaniment of music, does Hermione descend from her niche. Thus the ceremony is finally a celebration of Leontes' choice of a nobler course of action. In *Pericles*,

Cymbeline, and especially *The Winter's Tale*, wonder at the misfortunes of life is accompanied by wonder at human capacity to struggle toward the achievement of an ideal.

This struggle is even more prominent in the last two surviving plays by Shakespeare. I believe that in both *Henry VIII* and *The Two Noble Kinsmen* he collaborated with John Fletcher, with whom he is also thought to have written the lost play, *Cardenio*, but instead of advancing arguments here in favor of this view, I shall speak as if it were an accepted fact and only mention that there are some reputable scholars who disagree.[10] These two plays, different as they are—one a history play, one a romance—are strikingly similar in certain respects and have, for considerable periods of time, been similarly underestimated. *Henry VIII*, which has enjoyed a fairly continuous stage history largely because of the theatrical appeal of its pageantry, has, partly for the same reason, been regarded by many critics as unworthy of the sort of attention given to *Richard III* and the second tetralogy. In 1948 Frank Kermode opened a fine essay on the play with the remark, "Discontent is the chief characteristic of all criticism concerned with *Henry VIII*," and nine years later the Arden editor, R. A. Foakes, commented that "*Henry VIII* is still ignored in nearly all criticism of the last plays."[11] G. Wilson Knight, in *The Crown of Life*, he noted, was the honorable exception. Foakes him-

10. See discussions of authorship and conjectural assignments of scenes to the collaborators in *Henry VIII*, ed. S. Schoenbaum, 1967, reprinted in *Complete Signet Classic Shakespeare* (New York: Harcourt Brace Jovanovich, 1972); *The Two Noble Kinsmen*, ed. Clifford Leech, 1966; reprinted in *Complete Signet Classic Shakespeare* (New York: Harcourt Brace Jovanovich, 1972); all quotations are from these two editions; see also *Henry VIII*, ed. J. C. Maxwell (Cambridge: Cambridge University Press, 1962); *The Two Noble Kinsmen*, ed. G. R. Proudfoot, Regents Renaissance Drama (Lincoln, Neb.: University of Nebraska Press, 1970); Kenneth Muir, *Shakespeare as Collaborator* (London: Methuen, 1960), pp. 98–147; Cyrus Hoy, "The Shares of Fletcher and his Collaborators in the Beaumont and Fletcher Canon (VII)," *Studies in Bibliography*, 15 (1962): 71–90.

11. "What is Shakespeare's *Henry VIII* About?" *Durham University Journal*, n.s. 9 (1948): 48; reprinted *Shakespeare, the Histories*, ed. E. M. Waith (Englewood Cliffs, N.J.: Prentice-Hall, 1965), p. 168; *King Henry VIII* (London: Methuen, 1957), p. xlii.

self is one of several critics, including Kermode, who have helped to right the balance somewhat. *The Two Noble Kinsmen* has had only the briefest of stage histories. Davenant adapted it as *The Rivals* in the Restoration, after which it seems not to have been staged until this century. In 1908 Tucker Brooke thought it contained "no spark of psychological insight or philosophy of life which can in sober moments be thought either worthy of the mature Shakespeare or even suggestive of him,"[12] and more recent critics have rarely been much more flattering, if they have said anything at all about it. Here the notable exceptions are Philip Edwards, Clifford Leech, G. R. Proudfoot, and the most recent editor of the play, N. W. Bawcutt.[13] A very large percentage of what has been written about both plays has been devoted to the problem of authorship, and uncertainty on this point has clearly affected critical opinions.

The two plays resemble each other in being the most insistently ceremonious of all Shakespeare's plays. It is well known that one performance of *Henry VIII*, on June 29, 1613, was disastrously so, when the firing of cannon to signal the king's arrival at Cardinal Wolsey's banquet in act I set fire to the roof of the Globe and burnt it to the ground. If the ceremonial scenes of *The Two Noble Kinsmen* are less spectacular, they are no less numerous, and in both plays self-transcendence is the theme of a significant proportion of the ceremonies. In *Henry VIII* many of them are of the sort to be found in all the history plays, serving to remind us of the magnificence of the king and of the momentous importance of the deeds of kings and courtiers. But just here the concerns of history and romance intersect. Both history and romance often present somewhat larger-than-life portraits of their leading characters, and to this extent may resemble each other as varieties of heroic literature and drama. Talbot of *Henry VI, Part 1* would be at home in

12. *The Shakespeare Apocrypha* (Oxford: Clarendon Press, 1908), p. xliii.

13. Philip Edwards, "On the Design of 'The Two Noble Kinsmen,'" *Review of English Literature* V, 4 (1964): 89–105; Clifford Leech, introduction to Signet edition; G. R. Proudfoot, introduction to Regents Renaissance edition; N. W. Bawcutt, introduction to New Penguin edition (Harmondsworth: Penguin Books, 1977).

romance, and the Field of the Cloth of Gold, as described
by the historians and by Norfolk in *Henry VIII*, seems much
more like romance than an actual happening. Even though
Henry VIII does not belong to the category of exemplary
history, the most heroic kind, the prologue emphasizes its
concern with noble behavior:

> Such noble scenes as draw the eye to flow,
> We now present. Those that can pity, here
> May, if they think it well, let fall a tear:
> The subject will deserve it.

(11. 4–7)

The same might be said of many an Arthurian romance or
of *The Two Noble Kinsmen*.

Some of the "noble scenes" of *Henry VIII* are especially
suggestive of romance. A curious and striking feature of
this play, which repeatedly presents the fall of the mighty, is
the climb, sometimes steep and unexpected, of the principal
characters toward a lofty moral position. When Buckingham, the first to fall, is being led from his arraignment,
"tipstaves before him, the ax with the edge toward him,
halberds on each side," as the stage direction informs us (II,
i, 53 SD), he bids a formal farewell to the crowd that has
gathered, forgiving his enemies and asserting his loyalty to
the king. In the next act it is Wolsey's turn as he is arrested
and required to "render up the Great Seal." Suddenly de-
spising the "pomp and glory of the world," he now advises
his follower Cromwell to "fling away ambition" (III, ii,
441). Not only the rhetoric but the ceremonial occasions of
these farewell speeches call attention to the remarkable reformation of the two proud men.

Wilson Knight, commenting on the "poetry of conver-
sion" in *Henry VIII*, says: "The chief persons here show
regularly a certain graciousness, expressing, as persons, a
more than personal repose. The language of such self-tran-
scending is poetry and its active expression ritual . . . .
Ritual is an attempt to *live* for a while the higher, more
inclusive, life of poetry and drama, and therefore in its essence religious" (*The Crown of Life*, p. 319). Even if one
interprets the play, as I do, in a less religious light than does
Wilson Knight, one cannot miss the Christian emphasis in

another ennobling scene, where Queen Katherine at the end of her life forgives Wolsey and accepts her downfall and imminent death with serenity. Her state of mind is dramatized by a vision accompanied by "sad and solemn music":

The Vision

Enter, solemnly tripping one after another, six personages, clad in white robes, wearing on their heads garlands of bays, and golden vizards on their faces; branches of bays or palm in their hands. They first congee unto her, then dance; and at certain changes, the first two hold a spare garland over her head; at which the other four make reverent curtsies. Then the two that held the garland deliver the same to the other next two, who observe the same order in their changes, and holding the garland over her head; which done, they deliver the same garland to the last two, who likewise observe the same order; at which, as it were by inspiration, she makes in her sleep signs of rejoicing, and holdeth up her hands to heaven. And so in their dancing vanish, carrying the garland with them. The music continues.

(IV, ii, 82 SD)

Katherine is not converted, as are Buckingham and Wolsey. She has been admirable all along. Her final moments, nevertheless, show her on a higher moral plane than ever before.

The most striking ceremony of all is the baptism of Elizabeth, which not only provides a prophetic ending for the play but, by associating the king with the glories to come, confirms the more favorable view of his character presented somewhat unexpectedly in the last act. Henry, who has let Wolsey ruin Buckingham, has cruelly divorced the queen and then has consented to the fall of Wolsey when he discovered the cardinal's opposition to the marriage with Anne Bullen, behaves in a more judicious and regal fashion in saving Cranmer from the machinations of Gardiner and other members of the king's council. It is Cranmer, Archbishop of Canterbury, who, in an elaborate ceremony described in great detail in the stage directions, baptizes the baby Elizabeth and prophesies the glories of her reign. He goes on to speak of her successor,

> Who from the sacred ashes of her honor
> Shall starlike rise, as great in fame as she was,
> And so stand fixed.

(V, v, 45–47)

It is like the moment in a Jonsonian masque when some mythical figure points to King James as the embodiment of all the kingly virtues. Here this praise of the reigning sovereign is part of an awesome vision to which the king onstage responds:

*(ll. 63–
64)*

> O Lord Archbishop,
> Thou hast made me now a man.

If, as progenitor of this splendid future, Henry appears to be a far nobler person than the self-indulgent potentate of earlier scenes, the baptismal ceremony with the rhetoric of Cranmer's prophesy is mainly responsible for the elevation.

In *The Two Noble Kinsmen* the struggle for self-transcendence is expressed by a kind of ceremony which has its origins in the chivalric romance of twelfth-century France. Although most of the early romances have enough sex and violence to warrant a rating of Parental Guidance, the knights who are portrayed as admirable show a remarkable courtesy to each other and, of course, to ladies. Ceremonious forms of address are common; elaborate ceremonies govern behavior at court; and the *fine amour* which inspires the warrior involves him in a quasi-religious ritual. Courtesy, which underlies all these ceremonies, is a characteristic feature of courtly romance, where it is more highly developed and more insistently described than in the *chansons de geste*, the earlier heroic poems out of which romance developed. But as a component of chivalry, courtesy was also a feature of courtly life in the twelfth century and later. Hence the ceremonies of this sort of romance had a double life, in fact and fiction, as expressions of an ideal of behavior which was very imperfectly realized and yet was a powerful civilizing force. Since all such ceremonies are, in a sense, the contrivances of art—fictions imposed on everyday activities—their appearance in a story or play is doubly artful and their status as fact or fiction occasionally puzzling. We know, for instance, as we read about the tournament in *The Knight's Tale*, that procedures no less fantastic were followed in actual tournaments, but we also know that the portrayal of chivalry in such romances as this influenced those tournaments.

At the roots of the tradition of courtly, or chivalric, romance are the Arthurian romances of Chrétien de Troyes. No better illustrations of courtesy and its attendant ceremonies are to be found than in the opening pages of his *Erec et Enide*. The story begins:

One Easter Day in the Springtime, King Arthur held court in his town of Cardigan. Never was there seen so rich a court; for many a good knight was there, hardy, bold, and brave, and rich ladies and damsels, gentle and fair daughters of kings. But before the court was disbanded, the King told his knights that he wished to hunt the White Stag, in order to observe worthily the ancient custom. [14]

Clearly this is a formal occasion on which the worth of the Arthurian court is symbolically displayed by the dress and behavior of so many brave knights and fair ladies. The announcement by the king that he plans to honor an ancient custom gives importance to the occasion, prepares for another ceremony, and raises a disturbing problem. For Sir Gawain warns the king that since the killer of the White Stag must kiss the fairest maiden of the court, and since no less than five hundred high-born damsels are present, each with a knight prepared to defend her claim to be the fairest, the ceremonial kiss may end in a *mêlée*. The king has spoken, however, and the hunt of the White Stag is arranged.

Then Chrétien surprises the reader. Instead of enlarging upon the hunt he narrows his focus to one episode, which has its own ceremony. The queen and a damsel ride at some distance behind the hunters, where they are joined by Erec, one of the Knights of the Round Table, who was "very fair, brave, and courteous, though not yet twenty-five years old" (p. 2). His elegant apparel is described in detail. He carries no arms but his sword. As the three pause in a clearing, listening to the dogs, they see approaching an armed knight, lance in hand, accompanied by a damsel of noble bearing and preceded by a dwarf with a scourge—the sort of sight which was to become the staple of romance. When the queen sends her damsel to ask the knight to come to her, the dwarf, "who was rude and mean," as Chrétien tells us (p.

14. *Arthurian Romances*, trans. W. W. Comfort, Everyman's Library (London: Dent, 1914), p. 1.

3), strikes the girl's hand with his scourge. Erec is sent to insist that the knight come to the queen, but the dwarf blocks his way and, after an exchange of insults, strikes Erec on the neck and face. Since he is not armed, Erec prudently retreats.

A gross infringement of the precepts of chivalric courtesy is made all the more glaring by the exemplary courtesy of the queen and by the formal procedure of sending her envoys to issue an invitation. If the second invitation is more protest than politesse, it is still very civilized in contrast to the behavior which provoked it. Courtesy, as it was understood in the Middle Ages and the Renaissance, had something in common with the nameless virtue resembling friendship described by Aristotle in the *Nichomachean Ethics*. It is a mean between the excesses of those who always seek to please and those who are opposed to everything and are careless of giving pain. It differs from friendship in lacking passion or affection: a person acts in this way toward both strangers and acquaintances.[15]

But medieval courtesy was much more than this and was sometimes said to include all other virtues. Derek Brewer calls attention to its religious component, referring to the opening statement in an early fifteenth-century courtesy book for children: "courtesy comes from heaven."[16] According to the author of this treatise, it began with the greetings of Mary by the angel Gabriel and by Elizabeth. It is important to remember that the restraint which characterized chivalric courtesy was closely related to Christian doctrine and that chivalry as a whole had its religious side. Both secular and religious tradition, then, lay behind the doctrine of behavior loosely called courtesy. While good manners were sometimes narrowly seen as a sign of social status, they were interpreted more broadly as a manifestation of

15. See Aristotle, *The Nichomachean Ethics*, ed. R. W. Browne, Bohn Library (London: Bohn, 1850), 4:vi; Edmund Spenser, *The Faerie Queene*, VI and VII, ed. Edwin Greenlaw et al. (Baltimore: Johns Hopkins Press, 1938), pp. 325, 335.

16. *Chaucer in his Time* (London: Nelson, 1963), pp. 145, 204–37; *The Babees Book*, . . . etc., ed. F. J. Furnivall, EETS, o.s. 32 (London: Trübner, 1868), p. 16.

nobility of spirit. Thomist philosophy, indeed, would support the claim that nobility of spirit is worthless unless it is manifested in word and deed. In Wolfram von Eschenbach's *Parzival* the hero is bitterly reproached for his failure to give formal expression to his compassion by asking Amfortas the simple question, "What ails you?"[17]

The story of Erec and the discourteous knight next offers further examples of admirable behavior. Erec, who has ridden off in pursuit of the knight, is offered hospitality by a poor vavasor and his daughter. Chrétien describes the caring for Erec's horse, the serving of the meal, the conversations, and the preparation of the beds. Next day, armed by the damsel, Erec defeats the discourteous knight, elicits an apology, and obliges him to go with his damsel and the dwarf to throw himself upon the mercy of the queen. Knightly honor obliges him to do this, unaccompanied by any guard, just as King John of France once returned to prison in England when the hostages he had left behind broke parole and fled (Brewer, p. 156). Once the knight has done penance for the pride which caused his outrageous behavior, Guinevere forgives him and persuades Arthur to admit him to the queen's household. The episode ends with the return of Erec and the vavasor's daughter, who is instantly recognized as worthy of the kiss of the White Stag.

The ceremonies that crowd these opening pages go far toward revealing the character of life in the golden age of Arthur. There are rules for every activity from greeting or offering hospitality to defiance and combat. Compliance or noncompliance is a sure measure of worth, and thus ceremonies are often tests as well as expressions of this way of life. The queen's embassies to the strange knight demonstrate her courtesy as they test his and find it wanting. The combat between Erec and the discourteous knight is, of course, a test of valor, but in context it appears to be still more a test of essential worth and a means of reclaiming a lost sheep. The knight's formal apology in turn leads to the queen's generous gesture of forgiveness. The custom of the

17. *Parzival*, trans. Jessie L. Weston (London: Nutt, 1894), 1:144, 179, 280. The passages in *Parzival* were called to my attention by Margaret D. Waith.

kiss of the White Stag confronts King Arthur with the possibility of great dissension, but he shows his wisdom by deferring the kiss for three days at the queen's request. The arrival then of the vavasor's daughter, universally admired, makes the awarding of the kiss into an expression of unity. Each of these ceremonies offers the opportunity to reaffirm faith in the chivalric ideal.

The Trial of Chivalry, a turn-of-the-century play of modest artistic accomplishment, is mainly useful, like the earlier *Clyomon and Clamydes* and *Love and Fortune*, as an indication of the widespread interest in romance and of the way an uninspired dramatist may hit on ideas or techniques that a successor will use to greater advantage. The concerns of this play, as its title suggests, are very close to those of *Erec et Enide*, though the setting is pseudo-historical, during some war between the kings of France and Navarre. The play opens with a very grand scene in which the two kings, their sons, daughters, retinues, and armies enter at opposite doors with drums and colors to confront each other on a crowded stage. Defiances are exchanged. Then the French Prince Philip and Prince Ferdinand of Navarre kneel to their fathers to beg that "peace, not war, may end this difference" (sc. 1).[18] Bellamira joins her brother Ferdinand and Katharina her brother Philip. Though the motives of these young people are not totally unselfish, since Philip loves Bellamira and Ferdinand Katharina, it is evident throughout this play that peace is to be preferred to war, as is rarely the case in Elizabethan drama. The kings are being asked to raise their ethical sights. The two characters who seek to provoke war, one from each side to preserve the perfect symmetry, do so out of personal ambitions and lust. When the intercession of the princes and their sisters has resulted in a truce and the opposing forces have marched off, these two villains, Rodorick and Burbon, are left on the stage to concoct their plan for rekindling the war. The contrast is as obvious as that between masque and antimasque, and the staging of the scene of intercession has the ceremonial quality characteristic of the masque.

18. *A Collection of Old English Plays*, vol. 3, ed. A. H. Bullen (London: Wyman, 1884), p. 269.

A more subtle contrast is provided by one of the love plots: Katharina, loved by Ferdinand, loves his friend, the noble Earl of Pembroke. Ferdinand, knowing only that she is cool to him, chooses Pembroke as his spokesman. In the wooing scene, when Katharina makes her feelings for him transparent, Pembroke is a paragon of loyalty and honor, but when Katharina later reveals her preference to Ferdinand, he leaps to the conclusion that Pembroke has betrayed him. He obliges his reluctant friend to fight, and both are so seriously injured that each one thinks he has killed the other. It is hardly necessary to add that this is not true. One is nursed back to health by a forester, one by a fisher, but each one is still ignorant of the other's fate. Pembroke, loyal as ever, erects a tomb to the memory of Ferdinand, where by chance Katharina finds him in full armor (and hence effectively disguised). Showing her the tomb, he brings her to repentance for her cruel treatment of her lover.

The climactic events of this part of the story are as preposterous as they are spectacular, and yet they are undoubtedly ingenious as means of dramatizing certain chivalric ideals. For reasons which it would be tedious to enumerate, Pembroke and Ferdinand fight once more, their identities concealed by their armor. Mutual recognition comes soon, however, and they fall into each other's arms. The dramatic *pièce de résistance* follows when Pembroke persuades Ferdinand to pose as a statue of himself on the tomb. The repentant Katharina then arrives; Pembroke makes her admire the lifelikeness of the statue; she wishes that, like Pygmalion's statue, it might come to life; kneels to it; and, of course, it comes to life. Shakespeare probably knew this scene before he wrote *The Winter's Tale*.

Only one other moment in this "action packed" play need concern us. War has broken out between France and Navarre, but the wicked instigators of the conflict have been killed by Philip, Ferdinand, and Pembroke. Once more the two kings with their armies enter at opposite doors and exchange insults. Then between them enter the three apostles of chivalry, all of whom are supposed dead, and are unrecognized because their visors are down. After an impassioned plea for peace by Pembroke, the three reveal their

identities and kneel to the kings, who give up their enmity
and agree to the marriages of the princes and princesses; the
final ceremony of kneeling suppliants almost duplicates the
first. These scenes may have been in Shakespeare's mind
when he was working on *The Two Noble Kinsmen.*

Chivalry is a conspicuous feature of this play. As in
Chaucer's *Knight's Tale*, on which it is based, the opening
scene presents the plea of the weeping ladies. There Theseus, returning from "Femenye," where he has conquered
and wedded Ipolyta, has come almost to the town of Athens
with his wife and her sister Emelye when he sees kneeling
by the road "A compaignye of ladies, twaye and twaye,"
clad in black and "waymenting" in a most pathetic fashion.[19]
Finding that they are widowed duchesses and queens whom
Creon will not allow to bury the bodies of their husbands,
slain in the war against Thebes, Theseus alights from his
horse "with herte pitous," promises them to redress their
wrongs, and rides forth to Thebes (ll. 94–109). This eco-
nomical beginning is greatly altered for the stage. The first
to enter is a white-robed boy singing and strewing flowers
before Hymen, who is followed by a nymph, then Theseus
between other nymphs, Hippolyta, the bride, led by Pirithous, and attended by another nymph, and finally Emilia
with more of the wedding train. This procession is headed
for the temple where the wedding ceremony is to be completed. But suddenly the proceedings are interrupted by the
arrival of three queens in black, their veils stained. One
kneels before Theseus, one before Hippolyta, and one before Emilia. Each queen begs to be heard; each in turn is
told to rise; the first queen then describes their plight and
begs Theseus to intercede. He is moved but makes no promise. She kneels again, and he turns away. Then the second
queen urges Hippolyta to kneel for them, but she only
promises to "speak anon." The third queen, kneeling to
Emilia, speaks with such passion that Emilia assures her
Theseus' heart will melt. Instead, he orders the wedding
procession to move on to the temple. Each of the queens
speaks again, and he promises to help them soon. When the

19. *Chaucer's Poetry*, ed. E. T. Donaldson (New York: Ronald Press,
1958), 1. 40. All quotations are from this edition.

queens urge haste, he goes so far as to order one of his followers to raise a force "whilst we dispatch / This grand act of our life, this daring deed / Of fate in wedlock" (I, i, 162–64). The wedding still has priority. He argues that it is more important than all his previous deeds. But now Hippolyta kneels and is soon joined by Emilia. Only then does Theseus decide to defer his marriage in order, as Hippolyta puts it, "To do these poor queens service" (l. 198). The third queen says: "Thou being but mortal makest affections bend / To godlike honors" (ll. 228–29).

The reordering of events so as to present Theseus on his way to be married, the prolongation of the queens' begging, and the active participation of Hippolyta and Emilia turn the immediate display of pity by Chaucer's Theseus into a hard-won triumph of courtesy over self-interest, a movement toward more godlike behavior. The ceremoniousness of the occasion is greatly increased by having one ceremony interrupted by another; by devising the symmetrical arrangement of three queens addressing the three principal personages instead of a company of women lined up two by two; and by requiring the repeated gesture of kneeling. The scene in *The Two Noble Kinsmen* is strikingly similar in its broad outlines to the opening scene of intercession in *The Trial of Chivalry*, with its kneeling suppliants symmetrically arranged.

The next scene, which introduces Palamon and Arcite, presents the idea of the opening ceremony in a more straightforward piece of dramatic action. The cousins are so repelled by the degeneration of Thebes that they determine to leave the court of their uncle Creon. "'Tis in our power," says Palamon, "to / Be masters of our manners" (I, ii, 42–44). But when they are summoned by Creon to fight against Theseus, they decide that the defense of their city has a higher claim upon them than the search for a better place to live. Self-interest is again suppressed.

Two more ceremonies in act I mark the success of Theseus' generous enterprise. The first one, in scene iv, is prepared for by a prompter's warning in the margin of the text, thirty lines before the end of the preceding scene: "2. Hearses [in this case carriages] ready with Palamon: and

Arcite: the 3. Queenes. Theseus: and his Lordes ready" (I,
iii, opposite ll. 58–64). The stage direction at the opening
of scene iv indicates the sounds of an offstage battle, a re-
treat, and a flourish to announce the arrival of the victor.
Theseus enters with various followers and with the bodies
of the wounded Palamon and Arcite on hearses. Theseus is
met by the three queens, who promptly "fall on their faces
before him" to thank him. He sends them to find the bodies
of their husbands, and another marginal warning calls for
three more hearses to be ready. The main business of this
scene, however, is Theseus' disposition of Palamon and Arcite. Recognizing them as noble warriors whom he has seen
in the battle, he courteously orders that they are to have the
best medical attention and, though prisoners, are to be well
treated. The act ends with the "funeral solemnity" for the
husbands of the three queens, the bodies brought onstage on
the three hearses to the accompaniment of music.

The next act rapidly advances the plot: "the two noble
kinsmen" suddenly quarrel when they see Emilia from their
prison window and both fall in love with her; Arcite is removed from prison and banished; and the jailer's daughter
falls in love with Palamon. Only one scene is touched with
ceremony when the disguised Arcite, victor in some games
which are heard offstage, enters to a flourish of horns with
the ducal party. Proclaiming himself a gentleman and soldier out to seek fame, he is assigned to wait upon Emilia.

The third act contains the meeting of Palamon and Arcite
in the country and their interrupted fight. In Chaucer, Arcite
has risen "to doon his observance to May" with which he is
occupied as Palamon observes him from behind a bush (ll.
639–69). Shakespeare and Fletcher imagine a more public
observance, which Arcite describes as "a solemn rite," enacted by the Athenians in honor of May, "To th'heart of
ceremony" (III, i, 2–4). From time to time we hear horns
and "hallooing as people a-Maying," and eventually Arcite
hears the signal that a banquet is about to begin. While this
largely off-stage ceremony is progressing, Palamon, who
has been released by the jailer's daughter, enters "*as out of
a bush, with his shackles*" (a detail added by the playwrights), shakes his fist at Arcite, and addresses him bitterly

as "Traitor kinsman," "Falsest cousin," "A very thief," and the like (ll. 29–43). Arcite, however guilty he may be of duplicity, responds with remarkable courtesy, where Chaucer's Arcite "with full despitous herte" pulls out his sword (ll. 738–40). The marked contrast in behavior is the invention of the playwrights. In the face of continued abuse Arcite remains courteous to the end of the scene when, excusing himself, he leaves to perform his duties at the banquet.

When he returns later "with meat, wine, and files," (III, iii SD) in a scene which has no equivalent in Chaucer, Palamon is at first more friendly. As they eat and drink together they exchange reminiscences of earlier times until Palamon suddenly breaks out again, repeating the pattern of the prison scene, where friendship was abruptly replaced by enmity. Arcite refuses to give insult for insult, however, and after giving Palamon the file to cut off his shackles, leaves him as unfit for gentlemanly conversation.

Between this and their next scene together occurs a farcical little entertainment offered by a schoolmaster to the duke as he is hunting the next morning. It is an antimasque taken over with little alteration from Beaumont's *Masque of the Inner Temple and Gray's Inn*, where it is described in the argument as "a May-daunce or Rurall daunce, consisting likewise not of any suted persons, but of a confusion, or commixture of all such persons as are naturall and proper for Countrey sports."[20] The main masque, which follows, presents a sort of Field of the Cloth of Gold, with pavilions in which are placed fifteen "Olympian Knights." Encouraged by certain priests of Jupiter, the knights dance a few measures and are then called "to their *Olympian* games," for which they arm themselves with "Swords and Belts" (pp. 137–38).

There is a somewhat similar contrast in *The Two Noble Kinsmen*, where the rustic entertainment is followed by a scene in which Palamon and Arcite, with the utmost chivalric decorum, help each other into the armor that Arcite has brought from court. The scene is taken from the *Knight's*

---

20. *The Dramatic Works in the Beaumont and Fletcher Canon*, vol. 1, ed. Fredson Bowers (Cambridge: Cambridge University Press, 1966), p. 127.

Tale but strikingly altered in one respect. According to Chaucer,

(ll. 791–93)

> Ther nas no "good day" ne no saluinge,
> But straight, withouten word or rehercinge,
> Everich of hem heelp for to armen other . . .

In the play the long process of fastening each piece of armor in place is made strangely moving by the succession of polite exchanges: "O good-morrow!" "Good-morrow, noble kinsman." "Choose your arms." "Choose you, sir." "Is't not too heavy?" "I have worn a lighter, / But I shall make it serve" (III, vi, 16–17, 45, 56–57).

As they fight, the hunting party arrives, and Theseus orders them to stop. As in Chaucer, the revelation of their identities leads directly to Theseus' order for their execution. In about ten lines Chaucer tells how the queen, Emelye, and all the ladies weep and fall on their bare knees pleading for the knights until Theseus relents. Here is one occurrence of what is often called Chaucer's favorite line: "For pitee renneth soone in gentil herte" (l. 903). In the play it doesn't run so soon. Theseus condemns the knights to death and forbids anyone to speak for them, whereupon both Hippolyta and Emilia speak. Then they kneel. In alternate speeches they implore mercy "by our tie of marriage," "By your own spotless honor," "By that faith, that fair hand, and that honest heart you gave me!" "By that you would have pity in another, / By your own virtues infinite." "By valor" (ll. 196–200). Next Pirithous kneels and joins the two women in the invocation of ideals. Theseus hesitates, but argues for his edict. Emilia takes over the argument for a lesser penalty until finally Theseus says, "I feel compassion" (l. 271). Only then is the tournament arranged, as in Chaucer, though with several differences, the most notable of which is the stipulation that the loser and his supporters are to be executed. The spectacle of kneeling suppliants recalls the opening scene of the play, and the repetition of a scene of large-scale intercession once more recalls *The Trial of Chivalry*.

The prolonged softening of Theseus replaces a fine passage in the *Knight's Tale* describing his mental process. Theseus considers the power of love and of the instinct of self-preservation, mitigating the offenses of the young knights, and finally, moved by the weeping women, says to himself, "Fy / Upon a lord that wol have no mercy" (ll. 914–15). The stage action dramatizes this inward movement described by Chaucer's knight. In both cases Theseus approaches an ideal of knighthood. Chaucer sketches this ideal in the General Prologue in his portrait of the Knight, who "loved chivalrye, / Trouthe and honour, freedom and curteisye" (ll. 45–46). Talbot Donaldson's explanation of these words is illuminating: "In him the inward qualities of *trouthe* and *freedom*, fidelity to an ideal and largeness of spirit, find expression in *honour* and *curteisye*, honorable deeds and generous behavior" (*Chaucer's Poetry*, p. 882). The series of appeals to Theseus in the third act of *The Two Noble Kinsmen* seems to emphasize these same qualities. The two ceremonial intercessions with Theseus are therefore dramatic moments of central importance which define an ideal and portray movement toward it.

The most impressive of the ceremonies in the latter part of the play are those of the three prayers before the tournament in the fifth act, Arcite's to Mars, Palamon's to Venus, and Emilia's to Diana. With the three altars set up onstage all the principal characters but Emilia enter, Palamon and Arcite each accompanied by the three knights he has brought to support him. The kinsmen embrace and bid each other farewell; then the stage is emptied except for Arcite and his knights. As he prays to Mars they all prostrate themselves at the altar. The ritual is completed when the sound of clanging armor and "*a short thunder as the burst of a battle*" (V, i, 61 SD) answers the prayer. Arcite takes the signs "auspiciously" and leaves with his knights to be succeeded by Palamon and his knights, who go through a similar ritual and are rewarded by music and the sight of fluttering doves. Finally, to the soft music of recorders, Emilia enters in white, accompanied by her maids, to carry out a more elaborate ritual. A silver hind containing incense is placed on Diana's altar as Emilia prays to the "sacred, shadowy, cold, and constant queen" (l. 137). The hind vanishes under the altar to be replaced by a rose tree with a single rose on it (l. 162 SD), after which there is "*a sudden twang of instruments and the rose falls from the tree*" (l. 168 SD). The signs given by the gods, quite different from those in Chaucer, are all suitably mysterious, like Jupiter's message to Posthumus and the oracular prophecy in *The Winter's Tale*.

Once again the repeated act of kneeling is a memorable feature of the scene. The gesture of supplication here and elsewhere instantly conveys the idea of the helplessness of the suppliant as compared to a god or to a more powerful human being. When the appeal is addressed to a human being, the kneeling figures before him not only emphasize his superiority but also the demand that he use his power for the benefit of someone else, and thus rise to a higher moral level, "making," as the third queen puts it, "affections bend / To godlike honors." One gesture points to both limitation and transcendence.

The tournament of Palamon and Arcite is merely heard offstage. The remaining ceremony begins as Palamon, the loser, and his three knights are led, pinioned, to the scaffold. But, as they prepare to lay their heads on the block, Pirithous brings word of the mysterious accident that has befallen Arcite. Next Arcite, carried on in a chair, bestows Emilia on Palamon, begs forgiveness for his deception, and dies. Both Mars and Venus have answered their petitioners' prayers, Arcite's for victory, Palamon's for success in love, and thus, as Theseus says, "Have showed due justice" (V, iv, 108), but the main emphasis of the scene falls on sudden change, the subtle games of fortune, the childish inability of men to understand their situation. These are the subjects of the few final speeches and are implicit in the interrupted execution. Not attempting the Boethian consolation of Chaucer's tale, Theseus expresses thanks for what is and refuses to debate things "that are above our question" (1. 136). Philosophy is sacrificed in favor of a simpler and more easily dramatized wonder.

In Philip Edwards' persuasive interpretation the central idea of the play is a movement from innocence to experience. Again and again, as he shows, an early happiness is abruptly ended or changed. The import of the final ceremonies is consonant with this interpretation, while the earlier ones may perhaps be seen as adding a dimension to it. In this play, as in *Pericles*, what makes disillusionment affecting is the effort to behave nobly. The most memorable ceremonies give a brilliant visual immediacy to moments in which Theseus, Palamon, and Arcite make the choice of "honorable deeds and generous behavior"—"honour" and "curteisye."

7 Shakespeare's Stage Audiences
The Playwright's Reflections and Control of Audience Response
Alvin B. Kernan

Although the facts are well known, it seems still not to be
well understood that the English Renaissance dramatists,
Shakespeare included, were the first writers to work in the
marketplace situation which has since become the characteristic social and economic condition of the literary artist.
Before the late sixteenth century, poetry was not a profession but the expression of the talent and refined sensibility
of gifted, often noble amateurs, supported by private
means, as in the case of Sidney. Print was by and large
scorned as unworthy of the gentleman poet—none of Sidney's writings was published in his lifetime—and poetry
was circulated in manuscript among a small group of private
friends of similar tastes, as were Shakespeare's "sug'red
sonnets" and the poems of Donne. The existence of the
printing press and increasing literacy made it theoretically
possible for a writer to earn his living by writing for the
public, and Spenser and Shakespeare did print their poetry
in carefully edited editions dedicated to noble patrons. But
because of the stigma attached to print, because the reading
public remained relatively small, and because copyright
was not yet vested in the author, no writer—with perhaps
the exception of Thomas Nashe—was able to earn a living
by publishing until the eighteenth century, when the first
great man of print, Doctor Samuel Johnson, appeared.

But the building in London in 1576 of the first of many
English public theaters, the establishment of large resident
playing companies with star actors, the regular performance
of plays in the capital six days a week before large and var-

ied paying audiences, and the consequent need for a large number of plays which would attract an audience, provided for the first time a true marketplace for dramatic poetry. The economic historian Christopher Hill describes the new conditions in which art was produced in the theater in the following way:

> The way in which capitalist relations came to pervade all sectors of society can be illustrated from an industry not often considered by economic historians—the entertainment industry. . . . The financial genius of James Burbage brought playing from a small-scale private enterprise to a big business. . . . The drama was the first of the arts to be put on sale to the general public. Larger theaters brought bigger profits if the dramatist could draw his public. This created exciting new possibilities for the writers, though capitalism had its drawbacks too.[1]

I don't believe that Hill quite realizes how serious those "drawbacks" must have seemed to a contemporary writer, who, without preparation, was forced for the first time to think of his writing as work, of his poetry as a product produced for sale to the actors who controlled the theaters, bought the plays outright from their authors, and changed them at will. Nor were the authors familiar with a system in which their art became a commodity to be sold in a public place where its saleability depended on its attractiveness to a diverse audience with widely varying tastes drawn from all levels of society. The extreme self-consciousness of the English drama of this period—the prologues and epilogues, the direct addresses to the audience, the plays-within-the-plays, the internal dramatic discussions of poetic and theatrical matters—reflects the playwrights' continuing concern with the new circumstances in which they wrote and the multitude of questions raised by new economic and social circumstances about the status of the playwright, his relationship to the actors and performance, the ability of the theater to present the plays, and the social function of plays.

No question was more persistent or more worrisome, to judge by the evidence of the plays, than the nature and ap-

---

1. *Reformation to Industrial Revolution, 1530–1780*, The Pelican Economic History of Britain (Hammondsworth: Penguin Books, 1969), 2:89.

propriate response of the new theatrical audience. Poets
writing for a patron or for a small circle of friends were
addressing themselves to a limited group with shared values
and an educated interest in poetry, particularly its style and
its elegant expression of idealized themes in a manner approved by the courtly world. But the new audience of the
public theater was very different. First of all, it was large.
Alfred Harbage, in his remarkable and still authoritative
book, *Shakespeare's Audience* (1941), estimates that the
public theaters had an average capacity of between 2,500
and 3,000 people, that the average daily attendance in one
year, 1595, in the Rose Theater was about 1,000, and that
about 21,000 people, about 13 percent of the London population, went to the theaters in a given performance week in
1605—the one year for which he is able to work out the
figures. This is a mass audience, and if we take into account
all the varied evidence, it seems to have been a truly democratic audience, a cross-section of the population. Most
contemporary descriptions of the audience were written
from a hostile Puritan point of view and portray the "common haunters" of the theater, as Henry Crosse put it in
1603, in *Virtue's Commonwealth*, as

the leaudest persons in the land, apt for pilferie, periurie, forgerie,
or any rogories, the very scum, rascallitie, and baggage of the
people, thieues, cut-purses, shifters, cousoners; briefly an vnclean
generation, and spaune of vipers: must not here be good rule,
where is such a broode of Hell-bred creatures? for a Play is like a
sincke in a Towne, wherevnto all the filth doth runne: or a byle in
the body, that draweth all the ill humours vnto it.

This tradition of Shakespeare's brutal audience, idle appren-
tices, whores, pickpockets, swaggering soldiers, and ignorant rustics, has had a long life, but we know that the
audience also contained ambassadors, noblemen, foreign
travelers, gentlemen and women, students, and representa-
tives of all classes. Harbage, who believed that this public
theater audience was a true democratic and popular audience in the best sense, concluded that,

the audience as a whole understood and appreciated what it
bought and approved. Its approval could not have been easy to

win. . . . Shakespeare's audience was literally popular, ascending through each gradation from potboy to prince. It was the one to which he had been conditioned early and for which he had never ceased to write. It thrived for a time, it passed quickly, and its like has never existed since. It must be given much of the credit for the greatness of Shakespeare's plays.[2]

Harbage's view seems on the whole to be the more likely, particularly when we consider the fact that Shakespeare's remarkable plays were so well-received that they made him the most famous and the richest writer in England. But it would be most interesting to know how Shakespeare himself thought of and approached this new popular audience on whose response in the theater at the moment of performance the commercial and artistic success of his plays absolutely depended. The evidence for what he thought is, I want to argue, in his plays, though in a somewhat indirect form, and not easily interpreted. He did not harangue and instruct his audience directly like Ben Jonson, but he did often put an audience on stage in ways which suggest his conception of the relationship of playwright, play, actors, and audience. There are numerous brief appearances of stage audiences—Mistress Quickly and the drawers at the Boarshead admiringly watching Falstaff playing the part of the king, or Achilles laughing uproariously at Patroclus' parodying Nestor trying to don his armor, or Polonius admiring the elegant phrasing of the old play on the death of Priam, "that's good, 'mobled queen' is good"—and there are a number of references to audiences, such as the Prologue in *Henry V* encouraging the audience to let their "imaginary forces work," or Hamlet's description of a mixed audience containing both the "judicious" spectator, "the censure of which one must . . . o'erweigh a whole theater of others," and "the groundlings, who for the most part are capable of nothing but inexplicable dumb shows and noise."

On five occasions, however, Shakespeare puts plays-within-the-play on stage, complete with audiences, and examines in some detail the response of the audience to the

2. Alfred Harbage, *Shakespeare's Audience* (New York: Columbia University Press, 1941), p. 159.

performance and its effect upon them. Let us look at these
stage-audiences in chronological order and then see if we
can draw conclusions about Shakespeare's view of the audiences he worked for in the Globe, the Blackfriars, in various great houses, and in the Court, where his company presented his plays.

The first stage audience is Christopher Sly, the tinker in
The Taming of the Shrew, who is picked out of the mud,
where "like a swine he lies," dead drunk, and carried, for
the sake of amusement, to the house of a great lord. Here a
little pretense is arranged for him in which he is richly
clothed, waited on by servants, fed and wined, and presented with a fair wife in order to make him believe that he
is in truth a nobleman who has been mad for a number of
years and dreamed that he was a drunkard breaking up the
local alehouse. Sly has never seen a play before, thinking
that a "comontie," as he calls it, is like a "Christmas gam-
bold or a tumbling trick," but now he not only participates
in one, but serves as the audience to another, *The Taming of
the Shrew*, which is performed before him by a group of
traveling players. In the internal *Shrew* play, Petruchio
works on Kate in the same theatrical way that the lord has
worked on Sly, pretending that she is the opposite of what
she in fact is, sweet of voice rather than railing, inviting
rather than frowning, amorous rather than shrewish. The
result on both these most unpromising audiences is nothing
short of miraculous, at least in the simplest understanding
of the play, for Kate the shrew is transformed by theater into
a loving wife, while Sly the drunken tinker at least believes
he is become a lord:

> Am I a lord, and have I such a lady?
> Or do I dream? Or have I dreamed till now?
> I do not sleep: I see, I hear, I speak,
> I smell sweet savors and I feel soft things.
> Upon my life, I am a lord indeed
> And not a tinker nor Christopher Sly.

There is surely some naïveté here, some warning about the
danger of being so completely caught up in the illusion of
theater as to take it for reality, which is underscored in the

old play, *The Taming of the Shrew*, where Sly finds himself
in the end back in the mud again and sets off to tame his
shrew in the way that Petruchio handled Kate. But in Shakespeare's play, though Sly concludes his speech about being
a lord indeed with a request for "a pot o' th' smallest ale,"
he is left inside his transformation, and we are left to consider the possibility that even the crudest and most ignorant
parts of humanity may be improved by a play which shows
what man potentially can be.

Shakespeare's next stage audience, the young gentlemen
of the court of the king of Navarre and the princess of
France and her ladies in *Love's Labor's Lost*, are of much
higher social station than Christopher Sly but are a much
less satisfactory audience. The internal play to which they
are audience is "The Pageant of the Nine Worthies," that
"delightful ostentation, or show, or pageant, or antic, or
firework" presented in the posterior of the afternoon by several local rustics and pedants at the request of the king of
Navarre to entertain the princess. The Pageant is hideously
miscast—no more unworthy Worthies could be imagined—
and performed with epic inepitude; but what might only be
an embarrassing amateur theatrical made acceptable by the
good will of the actors and their desire to show off and
please their social betters is transformed into a complete
rout by the bad manners of the young noblemen in the audience. Perceiving the ludicrous gap between the preten-
sions of the clown, the schoolmaster, and the curate to be
Pompey, Alexander, and Hector, the young lords hoot at the
actors, interrupt their lines, argue with them, cause them to
forget their parts, drive them from the stage in confusion,
and bring the performance to an end by encouraging a fight
between two of the actors. The mild remonstrance of one of
the actors, Holofernes the schoolmaster, "This is not generous, not gentle, not humble," goes unheeded by the stage
audience, but it does remind the other audience in the theater of the responsibility that an audience always has in making even the most wretched play work as well as it can by
good manners, forbearance, and a tolerance born of sympathy for those who are trying to serve and entertain them.
In *Love's Labor's Lost* this sympathy is required not only

because it manifests the good manners required of any audience with a pretense to civility, but because in "The Pageant of the Nine Worthies" the stage audience is watching
an image of its own ineptitude. The young nobles throughout the play have also been "a little o'erparted" in trying to
play a series of heroic parts, philosophers searching for eternal fame through study, lovers, Muscovites, parts which
they have played about as foolishly as the rustics play their
pageant. Some humility about our own deficiencies as players of our own self-chosen heroic roles in life, Shakespeare
seems to be saying, ought to form a sympathetic bond between audiences and players, no matter how bad. We are all
players, and not such very good ones either, and the theater
is the place where we come face to face with our own theatrical selves. The experience if rightly understood should
make not for a feeling of distanced superiority but of identification and sympathy.

The stage audience is shown in this same perspective in *A
Midsummer Night's Dream*, where Theseus and Hippolyta
and the young lovers sit on their wedding night watching
Bottom and his company of artisans turned actors make a
"tedious brief scene" and "very tragical mirth" of a play of
Pyramus and Thisbe. The play is as bad as can be imagined,
"not one word apt, one player fitted," but Theseus has
learned the lesson that the young lords of Navarre had not,
for he knows the necessity of the truly noble-minded audience giving the players

> thanks for nothing.
> Our sport shall be to take what they mistake:
> And what poor duty cannot do, noble respect
> Takes it in might, not merit.

"Noble respect" also knows that the imagination of the audience must make up for the deficiencies of the players:
"The best in this kind are but shadows; and the worst are no
worse, if imagination amend them." But noble respect,
courtesy, and imagination of this audience cannot quite, to
use Theseus' word, "apprehend" *Pyramus and Thisbe* as
Bottom and his company play it, and so despite the best

intents the noble audience chatters away loudly during the performance, making cruelly witty remarks about the players, and calling attention to themselves and their own superiority. Their bad theatrical manners don't help the play—but then what could harm it?—and their self-centered inattention surely does not deprive them of any meaning of the play, for what meaning could it possibly have? So at least it seems on the stage; but from the auditorium, where another audience sits, the scene looks remarkably different. We see not a group of real people laughing at a group of wretched actors in a ridiculous play, but a group of actors somewhat deficient in the imagination needed to apprehend the fantastic world of love and fairies and magic they have moved through, watching, without any self-consciousness whatsoever, another group of actors without any imagination whatsoever completely missing the point of the mysterious story of love and tragic death they are trying to present. Since both the stage players and the stage audience are imaginatively deficient, taking their own sense of reality as absolute, the audience in the theater is inevitably reminded that they too may be somewhat too secure in turn in their own sense of reality and that full apprehension of Shakespeare's play, *A Midsummer Night's Dream*, and its fantastic events requires of us both good-mannered tolerance of its performance and some suspension of our own disbelief, some imaginative willingness to consider the play as an alternative image of the world, no more fantastic, no more make-believe, than the image of ourselves and our existence we call reality.

One of the major defenses of the English theater during this period was that it had a positive moral effect upon its audience, and in *Hamlet* Shakespeare tests this contention directly by showing the reactions of an audience to a play presented in the king's palace, the very moral center of the kingdom, before the king and queen and the royal court, and depicting a crime directly affecting the welfare of the state. The audience reactions to *The Mousetrap* or *The Murder of Gonzago* are so baffling and unexpected that critics and producers have consistently invented additional actions and motivations for the characters in the stage audience. But if we take the text literally, it is clear that we have here a variety of inadequate and unsatisfactory audience reactions to a play which presents a close parallel to the murder of the old king of Denmark by the present ruler. The queen, Gertrude, like the rest of the court who are later identified by Hamlet as "mutes or audience" to his death, gives no sign that she understands the relevance of the play to her own conduct or to events in Denmark. It may be, and is probably, as the evidence of the rest of the play suggests, that she knows nothing of the murder of her first husband, and that she is therefore unmoved by either the dumb-show or the action of the play depicting that murder. She is sensitive, however, to her "o'erhasty marriage," but when the Player Queen vows eternal faith to her first husband in terms unmistakably bearing on Gertrude's situation, she either misses the reference to herself altogether or passes it off with an easy remark—"Methinks the lady doth protest too much"—which suggests that the play has not bitten very deeply into her moral consciousness, as very little does.

Claudius does, of course, know what is going on, probably from the beginning of the dumb-show, which opens the play, and certainly by the time that the murder is acted out on stage and he rises in passion to call for lights. And in the best manner of the moral theory of drama, the staging of his crime forces him to look inward to his heart, and he retires to the chapel to examine his conscience and pray for his soul. But there he concludes that he cares so much for the kingdom and the queen he has stolen that he cannot give them up, and so he plots another murder to protect himself and secure his worldly gains.

Even Hamlet, who has such elevated theories about playing and the right kind of audience, turns out to be a most unsatisfactory audience. Like the young nobles who, to the often-voiced distress of the playwrights, often sat upon the public stage during performances to show off their fine wit and dress, he intrudes upon the play, baits the actors, criticizes their style, and comments in an audible voice on the action. Nor does the play have the desired moral effect upon him, any more than on Claudius, for while it confirms Clau-

dius' guilt, it does not cause Hamlet to sweep to his revenge. After a period of fury, during which he stabs Polonius by mistake, he allows himself to be led tamely off to
England. It can even be argued that Hamlet in his concentration on the literal meaning of the play and its bearing on
the political situation in Denmark really misses the more
general or philosophical meaning of *The Murder of Gonzago*, for the major portion of that play is taken up not by
scenes relating directly to historical events in Denmark but
with a long old-fashioned exchange between the Player
King and Player Queen about the failure of human purpose
in time and, in general, the lack of human control over fate.
Hamlet eventually comes to the point of view offered by the
Player King, accepting the divinity that shapes our ends and
the providence in the fall of a sparrow, but though this som-
ber view of fate and will is the center of the play the actors
perform in Elsinore, it is not what Hamlet hears or understands at the moment of performance. His own self-absorp-
tion and preconceptions make him a poor audience and
cause him to miss what the play might have told him.

Theatrical conditions are for once almost ideal in *The
Tempest*, where the playwright is a magician, his actors a
band of spirits doing his immediate bidding, and his audience so "charmed" that they accept the illusions he stages
for them as full reality. Through his art and his spirit-actors,
Ariel and his "meaner fellows," Prospero is able to stage
shipwrecks, emblematic banquets, a masque in which the
gods are revealed and speak to men, and a tableau in which
Ferdinand and Miranda play at chess. Through all these,
and Prospero's many other theatrical contrivances, such as
Ariel's songs or the animal chase of Caliban and his companions through the woods, the various "audiences" are perfectly protected from any real danger: "Not a hair perished.
On their sustaining garments not a blemish, / But fresher
than before." But so complete is the theatrical illusion of
reality on the magical island that the "charmed"—the word
most frequently used—audiences are "spell-stopped" and so
completely absorbed in the spectacles they see that they are
frequently drawn into the action. As a result, the playwright

is able to work his will on them and they experience fully and are morally transformed by the terror of shipwreck, the isolation of separation and exile, the wonder of the appearance of the gods of plenty. Ferdinand is brought to an understanding of the necessity for restraint and order. Alonso is brought to sorrow and repentance, and the playwright Prospero is brought by his own productions to forgive past injustices.

But even on this magical island, a geographic realization of Hamlet's "sterile promontory," where Shakespeare realizes his absolute "idea of a theater," the audience, like the playwright, theater, and actors, is finally not perfect. In their determined realism Sebastian and Antonio remind us of other Shakespearean stage audiences like Theseus and his court, or the king of Navarre and his companions, who through their unwillingness to suspend disbelief are unable to enter into the spirit of the play and are therefore unmoved by it. On the other hand, Caliban, Stefano, and Trinculo, the groundlings in every sense of Prospero's theater, are incapable of suspending belief, like Sly or Bottom and his fellows; and while they take the various performances Prospero arranges for them—for example, the dressing up in the stage costumes Ariel puts in their way—entirely literally, being "red-hot with drinking," they too are not transformed, though Stephano does, rather oddly to my mind, phrase one of the major lessons of the island, albeit in a somewhat imperfect way, "Every man shift for all the rest, and let no man take care for himself; for all is but fortune." The depressing effect of Caliban's literal-mindedness on theater is made clear when his approach with his fellows Trinculo and Stephano causes the Masque of Juno and Ceres to "heavily vanish," with "a strange, hollow, and confused noise."

It may even be, however, that there is an audience in *The Tempest* which knows even less of what takes place than Caliban's group. In *Hamlet* the prince identifies most of the Danish court as "You that look pale and tremble at this chance, / That are but mutes or audience to this act," and in *The Tempest* the mariners who remain asleep under hatches during most of the action seem also to represent a large general audience which experiences the terrifying and highly theatrical beginning of the play, the storm-scene, but doesn't know much of what takes place in the body of the play. They are, however, awakened and brought by Ariel to the happy ending at Prospero's cell in the center of the island, where, before sailing happily away, not much enlightened, they join in the general sense of reunion, forgiveness, and a better life ensuing. The Boatswain speaks for them all, and perhaps for the majority of all theatrical audiences, when in answer to Alonso's question, "how came you hither?" he speaks of a highly emotional but rather confusing spectacle which somehow moves from a frightening beginning to a happy ending:

> We were dead of sleep
> And (how we know not) all clapp'd under hatches;
> Where, but even now, with strange and several noises
> Of roaring, shrieking, howling, jingling chains,
> And moe diversity of sounds, all horrible,
> We were awak'd; straightway, at liberty;
> Where we, in all our trim, freshly beheld
> Our royal, good, and gallant ship, our master
> Cap'ring to eye her. On a trice, so please you,
> Even in a dream, were we divided from them
> And were brought moping hither.

Shakespeare knew very well what Ulysses tries to teach Achilles in *Troilus and Cressida*, in terms specifically suggesting the theater:

> no man is the lord of anything—
> Though in and of him there be much consisting—
> Till he communicate his parts to others.
> Nor doth he of himself know them for aught
> Till he behold them formed in th' applause
> Where they're extended; who, like an arch,
> reverb'rate
> The voice again, or, like a gate of steel
> Fronting the sun receives and renders back
> His figure and his heat.

This is what the playwright in the public theater, as well as Achilles the soldier hero, had to learn, and in his various presentations of stage audiences Shakespeare was obviously

trying to instruct his actual audiences in the part they finally
had to play in making his plays "like an arch, reverb'rate /
The voice again." By looking at images of themselves on
the stage, he seems to have thought, an audience could become self-conscious about its own role in making theater
work and learn the importance of simple good theatrical
manners: not talking while the performance is in progress,
not sitting upon the stage and making sneering critical remarks on the actors, not breaching the circle of theatrical
illusion, and, more positively, piecing out the crudities of
spectacle or performance with imagination and supporting
it with sympathetic understanding of the actors' desire to
please. But Shakespeare went far beyond these mild, and
usually humorous, remonstrances, for his stage audiences,
taken in total, are designed to make a real audience at least
consider, usually by means of negative example, the proper
way to approach and conceive of a play. To take it too literally, to take it for reality, like Sly, Bottom, Caliban and
even to some extent Hamlet, is to miss the real point and to
interfere, as these audiences always do, with the effective-
ness of the performance. To be too skeptical, however, like
the prince of Navarre, Theseus, or Sebastian and Antonio,
and not to allow the play even the status of temporary illusion, is equally destructive. Too much disbelief breaks off
Shakespeare's internal plays as frequently as too much belief.

To be fully effective and work the transformations of
which it is ideally capable, Shakespeare seems to be saying,
theater must be felt by the audience to be a fragile illusion,
at once real and unreal, requiring for its success not only
the art of the playwright and the skill of the actors but a
complex attitude on the part of the audience in which they
accept and are moved by the play as if it were real, while at
the same time knowing that it is not literally true. This theatrical epistemology, and the theatrical manners which are
required by it, are supported and enforced by what we might
call a theatrical metaphysic, which Shakespeare's internal
plays again and again put before the stage audiences and the
real audiences for their consideration. To put it most simply,

all Shakespeare's stage audiences are themselves necessarily actors in fact, finally no more real in their assumed
identities and actions than are the players and plays they
scoff at and interfere with in various ways. And while the
actors who make up the stage audiences are usually better
actors than the players in the internal plays, they are totally
unaware of their own status as actors, totally sure of their
own reality, and completely insensitive to the fact that they
have their existence only in plays which, while they main-
tain illusion more effectively, are no more real than the
oftentimes silly and ineffective plays-within-the-play which
they are watching. This perspective is maintained most subtly and extensively in *Hamlet*, where all the world, not just
The Murder of Gonzago, is "a stage / And all the men and
women merely players; they have their exits and their en-
trances, / And one man in his time plays many parts." But
it appears most obviously in *A Midsummer Night's Dream*
where Theseus, Hippolyta, and the young lovers sit laughing at Bottom and his company performing the wretched
Pyramus and Thisbe, totally unaware that they are themselves merely players in the Lord Chamberlain's Company
who exist in a play about Athenian dukes and Amazon
queens, lovers and fairies, of which many in the real audience would say, as Hippolyta does of Pyramus, "This is the
silliest stuff that ever I heard."

Since these stage audiences are images of the actual audience, Shakespeare has contrived matters in such a way as
to make the latter consider whether its skepticism about
Shakespeare's play may not finally be as unwarranted as
that of the stage audiences for the internal plays. Perhaps
we too, we are forced to see, are only players, unself-con-
sciously playing the roles of Smith and Jones in a larger
play we arrogantly title *Reality*. Once an audience's certainty about itself and its world is unsettled in this way, and
it is forced to consider itself as a group of actors, then it is
in the proper theatrical frame of mind, poised between belief and disbelief, to accept the fiction of the play as both
real and unreal. Real because it is worthy of consideration
as an alternate and possible image of the world, unreal be-

cause all images of the world, including the audience's, are
no more than fictions, the "baseless fabric of [a] vision." If
the revels end and the actors melt into air, so do

> The cloud-capped towers, the gorgeous palaces
> The solemn temples, the great globe itself,
> Yea, all which it inherit, . . . dissolve
> And, like this insubstantial pageant faded,
> Leave not a wrack behind.

It is an interesting fact that Shakespeare, reflecting upon
and trying to shape the response of the first large public
audiences that poets had to work with and for, should have
chosen to make his points by negative images. That is, he
never shows us an entirely ideal audience, though Theseus
expresses something like an ideal response, which he does
not live up to, in his comment on the actors: "The best in
this kind are but shadows; and the worst are no worse, if
imagination amend them." Earlier he gives fuller voice to a
noble view of audience ethics in his answer to the protest
that Bottom and company "can do nothing in this kind."

> The kinder we, to give them thanks for nothing.
> Our sport shall be to take what they mistake:
> And what poor duty cannot do, noble respect
> Takes it in might, not merit.
> Where I have come, great clerks have purposed
> To greet me with premeditated welcomes;
> Where I have seen them shiver and look pale,
> Make periods in the midst of sentences,
> Throttle their practiced accent in their fears,
> And, in conclusion, dumbly have broke off,
> Not paying me a welcome. Trust me, sweet,
> Out of this silence yet I picked a welcome;
> And in the modesty of fearful duty
> I read as much as from the rattling tongue
> Of saucy and audacious eloquence.
> Love, therefore, and tongue-tied simplicity
> In least speak most, to my capacity.

But most often the stage audiences are ill-mannered, im-
perceptive, and unchanged by what they see. They frequently reveal the effect of these attitudes on theater by in-

terrupting and halting the internal play before its conclusion. It may be that Shakespeare found that he could make his points about audience response and responsibility by showing what an audience should not be, which would, of course, make an audience more self-conscious than would the presentation of an ideal audience, with which we would easily and instantaneously identify, and consequently not become self-conscious about the role the audience has to play if theater is to succeed. But it is also necessary, I believe, to take seriously the fact that the playwright who pleased his audiences so well that he became rich and famous by doing so expresses in his plays only suspicion and doubts of an audience ranging all the way from groundlings, like Sly or Caliban, who are "for a jig or a tale of bawdry" and are "capable of nothing but inexplicable dumb shows and noise"; through those like Gertrude and the courtiers in Elsinore, or the mariners in *The Tempest*, who sit so uncomprehending at a play as to be merely "mutes or audience to this act"; to great nobles like Theseus and the prince of Denmark, who sits upon the stage making cynical remarks, dallying with his mistress, and putting the players out, "Leave thy damnable faces and begin. Come, / the croaking raven doth bellow for revenge."

While it seems inescapable that there is some distrust of audiences in all this, it is not certain that Shakespeare disliked and scorned his audiences, though we should note that such an attitude corresponds to the general sense of uneasiness about the public theater audiences expressed by the other dramatists of the time, most notably Jonson and Beaumont and Fletcher, but also Kyd and Marlowe. But we can come somewhat closer to glimpsing, while probably still not pinning down, Shakespeare's own feelings about his audience and theater by looking for a moment, in closing, at the standard configuration of his internal plays. In every case the play-within-the-play involves an upper-class aristocratic audience viewing with varying degrees of scorn and condescension a play, usually old-fashioned in style and awkward, or at least not totally satisfactory, in performance, put on by lower-class players, either amateur or professional. This structure appears most clearly in *Love's Labor's*

Lost, *A Midsummer Night's Dream*, and in *Hamlet*; and in
the latter two plays the philosophy or aesthetic underlying
the upper-class scorn of the players is made explicit: in Theseus' attack on imagination—"the lunatic, the lover, and the
poet"—and in Hamlet's speech to the players. The configuration is less apparent in *The Taming of the Shrew* and *The
Tempest*, but still in both cases there is an aristocratic presence, the lord who picks the drunken Sly out of the mud
and arranges both internal plays simply for his own amusement, and the duke turned playwright, Prospero, who even
while he practices his art scorns it as a "vanity" and an "in-
substantial pageant," refers to the players, Ariel and his
"quality," as a "rabble" of "meaner fellows," and in the end
abjures his "rough magic," breaks his staff, drowns his
book, and leaves his island stage to return to the more serious business of his dukedom in Milan.

The same pattern appears even in the briefer and less
formally bracketed internal plays in Shakespeare. The
Prince of Wales stands mockingly by while Falstaff, "as like
one of these harlotry players" as ever Mistress Quickly saw,
plays the part of the king in an old-fashioned style, "in King
Cambyses' vein." And Hal, of course, finds Falstaff's performance inadequate—"Dost thou speak like a king?"—and
goes on to play the part, superbly. Nothing seems more de-
basing to the queen of Egypt than that

> The quick comedians
> Extemporally will stage us, and present
> Our Alexandrian revels: Antony
> Shall be brought drunken forth, and I shall see
> Some squeaking Cleopatra boy my greatness
> I' th' posture of a whore.

Even in Shakespeare's *Sonnets*, which constitute an apology
for theater, the lower-class poet, "made lame by Fortune's
dearest spite," who must make his living writing for the
theater, since patronage has failed him, and find his life in
loving the Dark Lady, labors under the shadow of the noble
young man he tries to praise and the aristocratic way of life
and the courtly poetry it fostered.

If we want the historical equivalent of all this we need

only turn to Sidney's *Apology*, where from his aristocratic neoclassical perspective he describes a performance in the public theater and laughs at it for its mingling of kings and clowns, its greasy jokes, and its lack of unity. But, I think we should not conclude that the aristocracy and gentry were in Shakespeare's view the antagonists of the public theater, for we know in fact that the court and the aristocracy on the whole favored the theater and protected it from middle-class Puritan and City attacks. Nor should we conclude that Shakespeare was interested only in performances before the court and aristocracy, even though he never openly shows us a public theater, as Beaumont and Fletcher do in *The Knight of the Burning Pestle*, or Jonson in *Bartholomew Fair*. Rather, and here I will conclude, I think that in Shakespeare's paradigm of the theatrical situation, the aristocratic audience or presence represents an aristocratic artistic attitude towards the public drama, as is clear in Sidney, with which Shakespeare partly identified and which at the same time he opposed and criticized. The players and the play, on the other hand, have an equal ambivalence for him: lower-class, frequently awkward and "o'erparted," old-fashioned in style and subject matter, ludicrously inadequate in the inability to create the necessary illusion of great battles, gorgeous palaces, and solemn temples, they nonetheless in all their crudity are at least potentially capable of revealing profound truths, transforming human nature, making visible the farther ranges of reality, and telling us finally of the true nature of our existence as actors and our lives as plays. All this, if we will only see and listen in the right way.

8 Looking for Shakespeare
S. SCHOENBAUM

One scholar in his life gives many lectures. The series in which I have the honor tonight to participate is, however, quite different from what a speaker usually encounters on the circuit. It is sponsored not by public grants but by the personal donations of former students and colleagues who have chosen in this way to pay tribute to so worthy a friend and teacher as was Fred Tupper. The audience enlisted for these occasions is not limited to fellow specialists—there are enough such gatherings—but draws upon the larger university community and lay citizens of this capital city. Few subjects besides Shakespeare could hope to accomplish that ecumenical end.

I first heard of the Tupper lectures some years back when I lived in the Midwest, and the editor of a literary paper invited me to review *Shakespeare's Art*, which brought together the first set of lectures. Tonight the occasion is special in another way, for I cannot but be conscious that my address brings to a close the second cycle of eight lectures. Such an event, like the prospect of being hanged (to apply Dr. Johnson's remark), concentrates a man's mind wonderfully. In anticipation of it I have lately once again taken down from my shelf the volume edited by Milton Crane. Alfred Harbage gave the first of these lectures in the spring of 1965. Professor Harbage was my mentor when I was a callow graduate student at Columbia University during the handful of years he passed there before his translation to Harvard. By him I was initiated into the more removed mysteries of literary scholarship. He cautioned the novice not to cut his teeth on Shakespeare; he hadn't, himself. It was good advice, which I followed. Harbage left Columbia before I had completed my dissertation but invited me to send along the remaining chapters to him for evaluation, even though he would no longer serve on my committee. Only much later, when I had myself become a beleaguered director of dissertations, did I fully appreciate how generous he had been. His Tupper lecture, "Shakespeare and the Professions," conveys the flavor of this humanist's personality.

Professor Harbage has since passed from the scene. So too has the wittily urbane Terence Spencer, who followed him a few years later on this platform and spoke with polished care on Shakespeare's careless art. Clifford Leech, who lived his humanism, is also gone; he explored the dark theme of the invulnerability of evil. Other speakers—James McManaway, Madeleine Doran, and Maynard Mack—have since retired, laden with honors, from their academic or library posts. Were I to pick a personal favorite from among those Tupper lectures I know, it would, I suppose, be Professor Mack's subtly argued "*Antony and Cleopatra*: The Stillness and the Dance," with its closing burst of felicitous comparisons invoking Erasmus, Dante, Spenser, Keats, and Joyce, and its likening, as inspired as it is unexpected, of Shakespeare's Antony, "ever attracted by the sweeping magnanimity of his nature to an imagined literary world of perfect devotion between man and woman," with Cervantes's Don Quixote de la Mancha, suffering deeply yet a trifle comically "from the incongruities between the code he is attracted to and that world's demands."

All the speakers I have mentioned it has been my good fortune to know personally, some more than superficially, and that will perhaps account for my beginning with a backward glance. Another, more central, reason is that I have in mind a more familiar discourse than that usually inspired by a public forum such as this. Guided by memory and association, I propose to traverse some familiar paths. These are littered with artifacts: the perishable paper, parchment, and stone, which it is the historian's task to locate, examine, interpret, and then reinterpret. Those who have preceded me on this platform were, like me, looking for Shakespeare, and each in his own way found him. My own quest over the past fifteen years has been largely biographical. With the publication next year of *William Shakespeare: Records and Images*, the sequel volume to my 1975 *William Shakespeare: A Documentary Life*, I shall reach the conclusion of that phase of my scholarly pilgrimage. Bear with the infirmity of middle age, for I have, sometime since, slipped into my anecdotage. Yet I trust that some more general points about the persistence of the past will emerge to give a degree of impersonal substance to my personal remarks.

I

Let me begin my address proper by turning with you to a well-known and often reproduced ikon. I suppose just about everyone who has visited Stratford-upon-Avon has strolled over from the Birthplace or the Royal Shakespeare Theatre to the Collegiate Church of the Holy Trinity picturesquely situated on the Avon's banks and there stood before the Shakespeare monument executed by the Netherlandish stonemason, Gheerart Janssen, in Jacobean Renaissance style. The monument, situated in the north wall of the chancel, has a skull—a *memento mori*—at the apex, cherubs on either side of the cornice, and, between two columns, an effigy of the poet himself, plump of cheek and ruddy of complexion, looking for all the world like a burgher of Stratford such as a latter-day Rodin might with infinitely greater skill have depicted.

If the bust (more precisely, a half-length statue) commands little admiration for its aesthetic qualities, it presumably satisfied the expectations of those yet living who knew the dramatist and worshiped in Holy Trinity; more especially the surviving members of his immediate family: his widow Anne, who was eight years his senior and outlived him by another six; his daughters Susanna and Judith; and their husbands, Dr. John Hall and the ne'er-do-well Thomas Quiney. The Shakespeare in the chancel no doubt fails to confirm our romantic yearnings about what a poet should look like; but of course Shakespeare lived before Keats and Shelley and other Romantics had helped by their example to formulate that image. Some, indeed, have asked whether Shakespeare peers out from his niche in Holy Trinity not so much because of his artistic achievement as for the fact that he had become a man of property, owner of the second largest house in Stratford, not to mention 107 acres of arable land in Old Stratford. The Janssen who fashioned the Shakespeare memorial also executed, for installation in the same chancel, the monument, with recumbent effigy, of wealthy John Combe, old Ten-in-the-Hundred, as he was nicknamed for his usurious dealings. It was a Combe who occupied the biggest house in town. Or was Shakespeare memorialized, as others have suggested, because, having invested in Stratford titles, he was appropriately interred in the church as (in effect) a lay rector?

These are no doubt intriguing speculations, but the monument itself furnishes an answer to the question. The figure there, in his sleeveless gown over a doublet, has a pen in his right hand and a quire of paper under the left. He is not tending his accounts but is in the act of creation; for his mouth is open, apparently in the act of declaiming. The clumsy epitaph beneath, by who knows whom, confirms the symbolic posture, for the memorialist praises all "that he hath writ" as leaving "living art, but page, to serve his wit." And if Janssen's stonemason's shop was known to affluent Stratfordians such as the Combes, it must have also been familiar to Shakespeare's old fellow actors at the Globe, for it was situated only a short walk away on Bankside.

The bust in Holy Trinity is one of but two unquestionably authenticated likenesses, the other being the engraving, even clumsier, made by Martin Droeshout for the title-page of the First Folio. As such it holds a special interest for the biographer, who must, along with so much else, form an impression of what his subject looked like. Now, in studying the history of the monument, I came to the realization, which I must confess fascinates me, that the impersonal materials of biography have themselves biographies. In his eternizing sonnets Shakespeare more than once proclaims the power of his mighty verse to outlast material glories, whether these be tyrants' crests, gates of steel, or tombs of brass. The triumph of art over artifacts is a haunting commonplace and one which a minor poet, Leonard Digges, uses to wonderful effect when, in a commendatory poem to the First Folio, he prophesies that Shakespeare's works would outlast his own monument:

> when that stone is rent,
> And time dissolves thy Stratford monument,
> Here we alive shall view thee still. This book,
> When brass and marble fade, shall make thee look
> Fresh to all ages . . .

Digges' prediction may one day well prove true, but meanwhile we have both book and bust. The survival of Shakespeare's plays, despite the fact that their creator took no pains to ensure their preservation and that fully half remained unpublished when he died, must be reckoned little short of miraculous. So, in its own way, is the survival of his bust carved from soft limestone. Like the other evidences of Shakespeare's life, it has undergone vicissitudes since its installation.

That must have been by 1623, when the Folio was published; so much we know from Digges' poem. Our first record of a sightseer's impression was noted down a little over a decade later: a Lieutenant Hammond in 1634 refers to viewing in Stratford church "a neat monument of that famous English poet, Mr. William Shakespeare, who was born here."

In time the lively colors with which Janssen (in keeping with a long established tradition of funerary sculpture) had painted the bust faded, as the cold damp of Holy Trinity took its inevitable toll. The monument decayed. Fingers fell off; the alabaster architraves broke to bits. In 1746 re-beautification was commissioned and executed. Some years later a young gentleman who had "just emerged from Oxford"— he would less mischievously have stayed there—casually removed the stone pen from the poet's hand and, dithering, let it fall, upon which it shattered. Shakespeare has ever since held a replaceable quill. Before the century was out, Edmond Malone, the greatest Shakespeare scholar of his day, committed an act of singular folly when he arranged for the bust to be painted white, in keeping with his own neoclassical canons of taste. Eventually the paint was removed with solvents, and the bust repainted with colors suggested by recovered vestiges of the earlier paint. In 1973 vandals, entering the church by nocturnal stealth displaced the bust from its niche and perpetrated some minor damage to the monument. The police, understandably baffled, thought the intruders may have been looking for manuscripts by Shakespeare or one of the impostors to whom the plays are credited. If so, these malefactors seem to have gone unrewarded. So too have others who have slipped into Holy Trinity by night, armed with shovel and pail, seeking (like pirates after buried treature) the poet's bones or cryptic messages or elusive manuscripts.

With most of this history I was unacquainted when I paid my first visit to Holy Trinity Church. That was in 1964, the quatercentenary year, when I was invited to take part in the International Shakespeare Conference in Stratford. Late one afternoon I took some time out from the scholarly papers to visit the church. That occasion, to which I have alluded elsewhere, was for me unforgettable. In fact it amounted to what I can only describe as a quasi-mystical experience. The bust may not be much as a piece of sculpture but its setting is something else—there in the monument surmounted by the skull, in the chancel wall just a few yards from where Shakespeare lies buried under a slab with its famous malediction. One is overcome by strange emotions in the presence of the great and honored dead. One also feels, in this shrine at once holy and secular, a sense of the continuity in the veneration of so many pilgrims who have made this journey between the Shakespearean moment and our own. In any event, this adventure led me to set aside the work I then had in hand on Shakespeare's contemporaries to devote my energies to the biographical pursuit.

That quest has taken the form of a protracted odyssey, as I set myself the task of examining, firsthand, all the evidences for the study of Shakespeare's life—manuscripts, books, and artist's impressions—wherever these evidences are to be found. So, living in the Midwest, I was carried to both coasts, to the Folger Library here in Washington and the Huntington Library in San Marino, California; to the British Museum, the Public Record Office, the Guildhall Library, and Stationers' Hall in London; and in nearby Surrey to the College of God's Gift, which was founded by Edward Alleyn, who was (with Richard Burbage) one of the two great tragedians of Shakespeare's day. I visited the Kent County Archives Office in Maidstone, the Bodleian Library in Oxford, and the curious little repository known as the Plume Library in Maldon in Essex, founded by Thomas Plume, Archdeacon of Rochester, early in the eighteenth century. The Birthplace Records Office in Stratford-upon-Avon of course figured prominently in my itinerary, as did the Shakespeare properties there. I visited churches: in addition to Holy Trinity in Stratford, Worcester Cathedral, some twenty miles to the west, where in the muniments room one may still consult the documents relating to William's marriage to Anne Hathaway; St. Saviour's, where the playwright's brother Edmund, himself a player, was buried in 1607 with a forenoon tolling of the great bell, an event recorded in the parish register and fee book. Farthest afield was the University Library of Utrecht, with its unique contemporary sketch of the interior of an Elizabethan theater and unique copy of a panorama of Shakespeare's London, for such contextual materials also constituted part of my quest. A few items remain in private hands: a unique Elizabethan sketch of *Titus Andronicus* in performance, in the library of the Marquess of Bath at his stately home at Longleat; an account book entry, curious in nature, of a payment to Shakespeare for devising an *impresa*—an insignia with motto, to be painted on a paper shield for the sixth Earl of Rutland, and carried by him as he rode on horseback for a tourney at Court on the King's Accession Day in 1613—a record still at Belvoir Castle, seat of the Rutlands, in the Peak District of Derbyshire.

These remains and others I personally examined not once but on two separate occasions, first when I was gathering my materials and then again when I was provided with proof copies of facsimiles to check against the originals for fidelity of reproduction. My obsessive-compulsive undertaking, then, has been a long one.

What conclusions may in retrospection—for my humor tonight is retrospective—be drawn from the long obsessive-compulsive pursuit? The first is that one's naïve sense of awe, which five years back I savored in a preface, dies hard. These sometimes fragile artifacts have survived the accidents of history—neglect, burial, collective amnesia, wars, fires, flood, and pestilence, and depredations of miscreants and the misguided ministrations of would-be preservers. One may still hold the paper or vellum in the hand. They both satisfy and stimulate curiosity.

Thus we have Shakespeare's will, brought to light over a century after he passed from the scene. It has been endlessly studied, but we still puzzle over the significance of omissions: no mention of the Earl of Southampton, to whom Shakespeare dedicated two youthful poems and who was still alive when the poet died, or for that matter any other noble lord; no mention of any Hathaways, members of his wife's tribe. Above all, students debate the notorious bequest of the second-best bed to the widow. We study the three Shakespeare signatures, one at the bottom of each of the three sheets, and ponder the actual condition of the testator who declares, in the conventional phraseology of such instruments, "In the name of God, amen, I William Shakespeare . . . in perfect health and memory, God be praised, do make and ordain this my last will and testament."

Or to take a less celebrated example. A single letter addressed to Shakespeare survives. It surfaced in 1793 when Malone came upon it in a bundle among thousands of documents in the Stratford archive. It is today in the Birthplace Trust Records Office. The letter was addressed by Richard Quiney to "his loving good friend and countryman Mr. Wm. Shakespeare" in October 1598. By occupation a mercer, Quiney was the scion of a respected Stratford family, the essence of the solid citizen. What manner of business had he with the playwright who had not long since given the London stage *Romeo and Juliet*, *The Merchant of Venice*, and *Henry IV* with Prince Hal and Falstaff? The gist of the communication is an appeal for a loan of £30 on good security. In a time when a skilled artisan pulled down sixpence for a day's labor and an ordinary schoolmaster might earn

£10 in a year, £30 represented a considerable sum. So Richard Quiney's letter, while anything but poetical, tells us something of interest, for it makes clear that by late 1598, when Shakespeare was thirty-four, he impressed his well-placed Stratford neighbor as being himself sufficiently well placed to be a likely target for a far from trifling loan. In the annals of versifying, how many poets anywhere have been so regarded by their mid-thirties? At any age? (I am reminded of a skit some years back on *Monty Python's Flying Circus* celebrating the career of a Scottish poet. One of this bard's early epics began something like, "O, can ye let me have a fiver?" Later, having established himself, another epic began. "Can you let me have ten pounds?") Quiney now and then found himself in London, so we can speculate on whether he knew Shakespeare as the darling of stage-land. Maybe the mercer did, but I rather doubt it. More likely he was aware that Shakespeare had lately bought a mansion house in Stratford.

Thus far clear sailing as we ponder Richard Quiney's letter. But as so often with the Shakespeare records, a tantalizing question presents itself. Why was this rapidly set-down document—so we gather from the hand—found among the Quiney papers in Stratford? He must then not have dispatched it. Why not? Did he decide against the overture? Or did he have a personal encounter with the dramatist and accomplish his business then? Your guess is as good as mine. The paper at once presents and withholds information. This is the Shakespeare biographer's constant vexation.

The Quiney letter, fragile and in its own way mysterious, illustrates the miracle of preservation. My next sample reflects some of the vagaries which may attend the miracle, and I have chosen this particular one because I myself had a supporting role in the dénouement. My Shakespearean quest early took me to the Folger Library. I don't remember precisely when my visit took place, nor who it was I encountered behind the reference desk in the Reading Room. But I recall this amiable young librarian's responding with surprise when I explained that I had come to see the Blackfriars Gate-house conveyance. Now, this gate-house, situated in a fashionable residential district not far from the

Blackfriars Theatre which Shakespeare's company, the King's Men, used from 1609 as their winter playhouse, represents, so far as we know, the last investment made by the dramatist before his death. He bought the property in March 1613, very likely after he had retired from the stage to pass his twilight days in his native Stratford. Once again a Shakespeare record raises questions, for the financial arrangements would seem to have excluded the widow's hereditary claim on the Blackfriars Gate-house. As elsewhere, alternative interpretations are available; but the matter is too complicated to explore here. I am concerned now merely with the physical existence of this legal instrument. Two copies survive. One, bearing Shakespeare's signature, is in the Guildhall Library in London. This was no doubt the seller's copy. Its counterpart at the Folger does not bear Shakespeare's signature, presumably because it was the copy retained by the purchaser, whose own signature on the document in his possession would serve no useful legal purpose. The Folger version of the conveyance therefore has a special interest as being one of the few existing documents we can reasonably assume to have once been in Shakespeare's own possession. Probably he kept it at New Place, for the Blackfriars Gate-house seems to have been acquired as an investment rather than to serve as his residence.

James Orchard Halliwell-Phillipps, arguably the greatest of Victorian Shakespeare scholars, obtained the purchaser's counterpart in 1872. Eventually, after Halliwell-Phillipps' death, it passed into the collection of Henry Clay Folger and thus found a place in the library that bears his name. The librarian having recovered from my request, the conveyance was brought to me in the quaint wooden box in which, I suppose, Halliwell-Phillipps had kept it in his equally quaint Shakespearean wigwam at Hollingbury Copse. The box was very small but the document, as is in the nature of such instruments, very large; so evidently it had been folded many times before insertion. "How very nice!" I exclaimed. "And now may I see this curiosity?" But the box was locked. Where, then, had the key gone? A frantic search took place. No key. Finally a locksmith was fetched. He scratched his head. His services had frequently been sought after burglaries or fits of absentmindedness, but he had never encountered such a box with so tiny a Victorian lock. After some desultory efforts the locksmith gave up. Finally, with a sweepingly impatient gesture, my benefactress behind the Reading Room desk removed a bobby pin from her neatly coiffed hair, inserted it in the lock, and—presto!— the box delivered its contents. "Splendid!" I said, not for the first time that day. I removed the precious vellum and began to unfold it. Alarm. Was it safe, after the passage of God knows how many years, to tamper with the configuration of the document? Might it not possibly fall to bits? I pointed out that a record, even a unique one, that could not be studied was of little use to anyone. And so I was allowed to go ahead. I unfolded it without incident and examined the corrugated surface. "Let us now photograph it," I suggested. Silence, and again consternation. To photograph it, somehow we would have to contrive to make it lie flat and maybe even have to stick pins in the four corners. This too we accomplished, apparently without pins, and the Folger photographic department produced a picture of superlative quality. Whatever else might in future happen, we now had a permanent and consultable record.

As far as I know, the Blackfriars Gate-house conveyance once in Shakespeare's hands has never been returned to Halliwell-Phillipps' box, although I am informed that the library has retained that curiosity. Right now the conveyance has temporarily migrated to Kansas City, where it forms part of the great Folger traveling exhibition, "Shakespeare: The Globe and the World," at the Nelson Gallery. When in Kansas City I mosied over to have a peek. The Blackfriars Gatehouse conveyance has never, I suspect, looked better at any time since when it was first drawn up. For to prepare it for display, the wonderfully able Folger conservator, Frank Mowery, had the document benevolently stretched on the rack. Visitors to the Nelson Gallery cluster round and gape at the apparently pristine surface.

Not every story has a similarly happy ending. Time, like Shelley's west wind, is destroyer as well as preserver. Two Quiney letters, not addressed to Shakespeare but referring to him, have for long been well known to students. These, like the one from Richard to his loving countryman, are in the Birthplace Records Office. On one of my visits to that hospitable archive I discovered with alarm that these Quiney letters had suffered irreparable damage during the last war. Because of the bombing of nearby Coventry, the custodians had placed them, as a protective measure, in the basement of the Records Office, which is a few steps down from the Birthplace in Henley Street. There a water leak developed which, by a remarkable stroke of bad luck, singled out these two papers from among the many bound together in a thick volume. As a result these documents were rendered illegible. The ultra-violet lamp helped a bit in bringing out some of the properties of the ink, but not enough to make the writing legible. I suggested infra-red examination, which possibly would reveal other properties; but the nearest lamp was some miles away in Oxford, and the Birthplace authorities were understandably reluctant to risk additional calamity by having the volume transported. No earlier photographs of these Quiney letters were on file in the Records Office, nor did the staff have any information that photographs had been taken. Some time later, when back at the Folger, I came quite by chance upon one of those collections published in the last century in limited editions by the indefatigable Halliwell-Phillipps; it contained a facsimile, made from a tracing, of a key passage from one of the two letters. Not much of a consolation, but surely better than nothing.

To cite another, more crucial, example, six signatures by Shakespeare survive, three of them in the will, plus two short monosyllables, "By me," also in the will; that is all we have with certainty in the poet's own hand, although many today believe (partly on paleographical grounds) that three pages from the manuscript play of *Sir Thomas More* in the British Library are Shakespeare holograph. The signature on the second sheet of the will is badly eroded and has been for some time. A facsimile, also made from a tracing, was published in the eighteenth century, when the signature was more legible, and this is of some limited help. But I made an unsettling discovery when I compared the bottom of this second sheet in a photographic facsimile published in 1916 with a more recent photograph. This comparison revealed that at least a half inch of the precious document has disappeared from the bottom. If time is the west wind, it is also (to vary the figure) a mouse, and documents are the cheese it nibbles.

An obvious moral may be drawn from these cautionary tales. Every collector, private or institutional, should safeguard the historical record—I am not now speaking about the artifacts themselves—by having whatever is unique photographed. And not only the self-evidently precious items, because who knows for sure what will stir, as unexpected revelation, the historian of the future? As for the artifacts, it goes without saying that we must avail ourselves of the most sophisticated technology when it comes to temperature and humidity control. The Folger Shakespeare Library last year closed its doors and will remain shut for at least a year longer as renovation proceeds. Readers will find the new facilities more comfortable than the old, but it was mainly the comfort of the manuscripts and books that was being consulted when plans were approved. It was with their comfort uppermost in mind that I, as a trustee of the Folger, voted in favor of the rebuilding program, although I knew that that program would deprive me of the materials for my research at a crucial time, materials for access to which I had lately transplanted myself to Washington. First things first.

Thus far my examples, while endlessly discussable, are familiar to most students. What, we may ask, is the shape of things to come? Will the future yield further documentary discoveries to elucidate Shakespeare's life, or have we reached the end of the line? If we haven't, what form are new findings likely to take? Prognostication is an uncertain art, and I can claim no special powers as a seer, but I believe I can answer with reasonable confidence, yes, we will add to the store, although I doubt that the revelations to come will be of the magnitude of the marriage license bond or the will. "The picture of Shakespeare's life in Warwickshire," Mark Eccles has written, "is a mosaic with most of the pieces missing." What we can hope to do is to recover some of the pieces—for the London as well as the Warwickshire

mosaic—and make the picture a little more complete. Such
recovery is in fact a continuing process. The quatercentenary year saw the announcement of two discoveries from the
Sackville papers on deposit in the Kent County Archives
Office in Maidstone. These records come from the Stratford
ecclesiastical court. The first shows that Shakespeare's elder
daughter Susanna was cited in May 1606 for failure to receive communion the preceding Easter. Such a citation normally suggests Catholic sympathies, and so it may shed
some light on the much disputed topic of the poet's religious
leanings. But like so many other Shakespeare records, it
teases as well as satisfies curiosity, for John Hall, the husband Susanna took in 1607, was a respected physician with
pronounced Puritan leanings. The second item records the
hearing and conviction of Shakespeare's other son-in-law
Thomas Quiney for sexual intercourse with a Margaret
Wheeler. Quiney admitted the offense, was lightly fined,
and ordered to acknowledge his crime before the minister
of nearby Bishopton—a lenient substitution for public penance. That was on March 26, 1616, less than a fortnight
after Margaret Wheeler died with the infant in childbirth
and was buried in the churchyard of Holy Trinity. Thomas
Quiney's delinquency confirms what biographers have long
suspected, that Shakespeare was concerned about his unsatisfactory new son-in-law, who married Judith Shakespeare
in February 1616, on the eve of his disgrace and just two
months before the dramatist's death. Did the small-town
scandal of the Margaret Wheeler affair, with its grim after-
math, hasten his decease?

II

So we have lots of Shakespeare records. Yet popular
opinion insists that we know almost nothing about Shakespeare, that a postcard will sum up knowledge, with plenty
of room left for the address. I hear this sort of thing all the
time as part of academic or theatrical chitchat, chitchat
which demonstrates that small-talk can approach the infini-
tesimal. Popular opinion, then, is wrong. Or maybe it is
wrong in one sense but in another, more profound, way cor-

rect. For what we know about Shakespeare the man belongs
almost entirely to the public record of formal occasions. He
required certain documents in order to marry. His christen-
ing and burial were duly entered in his church's parish registers. So too were the baptisms of his three children, the
marriages of the two daughters, and the burial of all three
offspring, most poignantly that of his son Hamnet at the age
of eleven. They do not tell us whether the London playwright attended the Stratford funeral of his only boy, let
alone how he felt about this real-life tragedy. Other records
chronicle Shakespeare's professional life: his connections
with his acting company, the printing—or not printing—in
his lifetime of his plays and poems. The rest have mostly to
do with the acquisition of houses and other property and the
prudent provision made for the estate after Shakespeare's
decease. They show no concern about what would become
of his achievement as an artist. In a collection of short stories and other writings entitled *Labyrinths*, Jorge Luis
Borges calls his meditation on Shakespeare "Everything and
Nothing." In his life he seems to have been nothing, at least
not anybody very special, although he was materially much
more successful than most.

The life record thus seems to offer no insight into how
the transient stuff of life was metamorphosed into transcendent achievements of art. We know that some successful
writers have sought to discourage prying inquiry into their
happy or sullen craft. Somerset Maugham is a recent instance. In his will he took pains—of course unsuccessful—
to ban any biographies and asked that his letters be destroyed. Shakespeare did not even bother to do that. That
aloofness—or, more probably, indifference—has served
only to whet all the more the appetite for letters or diaries.
These we have been sometimes offered.

There is time here tonight for only one example. In 1811
"A Barrister"—that is how the author's name appeared on
the title page—published *A Tour in Quest of Geneaology,
through several parts of Wales, Somersetshire, and Wilt-
shire, in a Series of Letters to a Friend in Dublin; inter-
spersed with a Description of Stourhead and Stonehenge;
together with Various Anecdotes, and Curious Fragments*

from a Manuscript Collection Ascribed to Shakespeare. I will not trouble you with the barrister's description of Stonehenge, but the manuscript collection invites notice. "The most interesting portion of it [the author tells us] consists of letters that passed between him, Sir Christopher Hatton, Sir Philip Sidney, Lord Southampton, Richard Sadlier, Henry Cuffe, &c.; part of a journal, like most journals, carried on for a month together, then suspended during a period of four or five years; and memoirs of his own time written by himself. Some of the items are uncommonly curious, as they give you not only the costume [*sic*] of the age he lived in, but let you into his private and domestic life, and the rudiments of his vast conception."

A couple of diary items must here suffice. One tells us how Shakespeare was almost tempted to excise a celebrated passage from one of his most celebrated plays: "Att the requeste of a ladie of honore, noe less a parsonage than the Countesse of Pembrok, I had dropped the grave sceane in mie Hamlett, butt the poppulece grew outraigiouse, and threatted to bury us all unlesse theire favorit parte was restoried." Another purports to reveal how Shakespeare took up language study: "Having an ernest desier to lerne forraine tonges, it was mie goode happ to have in mie fathere's howse an Ittalian, one Girolamo Albergi, tho he went bye the name of Francesco Manzini, a dier of woole; but he was not what he wished to passe for; he had the breedinge of a gentilman, and was a righte sounde scholer. It was he tought me the littel Italian I know, and rubbid up my Lattin; we redd Bandello's Novells togither, from the which I getherid some delliceous flowres to stick in mie dramattick poseys. He was nevew to Battisto Tibaldi, who made a translacion of the Greek poete, Homar, into Ittalian, he showed me a coppy of it givin him by hys kinsman, Ercolo Tibaldi." There are others: How flea infestation presented its problems, how the Earl of Southampton spoke of *Richard III* with high praise when he returned the unfinished tragedy in April 1595—a date that would enforce some changes in our received ideas about the Shakespeare chronology.

The barrister author of the *Tour in Quest of Genealogy* was, we know from other sources, Richard Fenton, and,

although he tells us that he toyed with the idea of publishing
the whole of Shakespeare's memoirs, he produced no more
than bits and pieces of "this curious farrago." Others besides
Fenton have beguiled readers with purported revelations.
Some, like William-Henry Ireland and John Payne Collier,
sent shock waves through the literary establishments of their
day. But the Ireland forgeries—the love letter to dearest
Anna; the deed by which Shakespeare bequeathed his
manuscript plays to (with wonder let it be said!) an Elizabethan William Henry Ireland, his chum; and the rest—
these forgeries were no more than the rationalized fantasies
of an emotionally retarded youth not yet twenty. The Collier
impostures offered "evidence" in support of pet theories
which otherwise he would have had difficulty in proving,
because they were wrong. The Fenton fabrications caused
scarcely a ripple. Even were any of these contributions
genuine, they would not begin to answer the overwhelming
question posed to the biographer of Shakespeare: How
could this apparently ordinary man have created these su-
preme works?

To such a question no answer is really possible. How,
under the most ideal circumstances, could biography render
the inconceivable comprehensible? True, biography has its
own art, but it is, by and large, a prosaic endeavor. When
imaginative artists have made Shakespeare a character in
their plays and novels—and many have done so—they have
taken full advantage of the liberty of interpretation offered
them and given free reign to intuitive invention; but although their creations sometimes have an interest of their
own (I think, for example, of Anthony Burgess' *Nothing
Like the Sun*) they do not in any profound way furnish the
illumination we crave.

So we have to make do with what we have. Surely it is
the seemingly antipodean contrast between the man, as we
know him, and the work that lies at the source of the anti-
Stratfordian heresies: the theories offering Lord Francis Bacon or the seventeenth Earl of Oxford or the sixth Earl of
Derby or any of the rest as an alternative to the grammar-
school-educated glover's son from Stratford—as though a
university degree and blue blood explained anything. The

very term *heresy* implies, as its converse, unquestioning religious faith; the biographer must contend with the added
burden of generations of bardolatry. Were we by some miracle to recover the original script, rough draft or fair copy,
of *Hamlet* in Shakespeare's own hand, how many of us
would, like Rossini confronted with the holograph of Mo-
zart's *Don Giovanni*, fall weeping to our knees, and kissing
the yellowed pages, cry out, "He was God Himself."

Be that as it may, there is ample precedent for the god
becoming vulnerably mortal. For godlike politicians that is
usually the prudent course. A feature in *Time* magazine
(February 4) analyzes Ronald Reagan's also-ran finish on
the Iowa Republican primary. When the governor was leading in the polls, he kept aloof from the battle. John Sears,
"his highly touted strategist," explained, "It won't do any
good to have Reagan going to coffees and shaking hands
like the others. People would get the idea that he's an ordinary man like the rest of us."

An ordinary man like the rest of us. Reagan has since
learned his lesson well. Shakespeare never needed to learn
it. In him the ordinary becomes extraordinary, the extraordinary ordinary. Does not that paradox yield its own in-
terpretive clue to the mystery we are exploring? Is not much
of what is fundamental to Shakespeare's art the ordinary—
the bread and cheese of life—hugely, astonishingly magnified by his unique gifts? *Romeo and Juliet* is an obvious
example: young love, parental disapproval, the generation
gap. We've heard it all before; we'll hear it all again. But in
Romeo and Juliet the parents are locked into a murderous
ancient feud, the sources of which have long since become
obscure even to the antagonists. The divisions between the
families and between young and old exact their fearful
price. If the conflicts are a staple of popular romance, the
degree—the magnification—is exceptional, as is the lyricism and incandescence with which it is realized. The
ordinary has become extraordinary. Such is the alchemy
of art.

We see an analogous alchemy operating everywhere in
Shakespearean tragedy. Bear with me if my examples appear outrageous. How many domestic dramas and sit-coms

draw upon comings and goings among gray-flanneled cor-
porate types in executive suites, the Madison Avenue annex
to the corridors of power? The power-seekers compete and
bring their problems home to their spouses; indigestion and
insomnia result. The hero is a middle-level executive. He is
ambitious, his wife even more so and keen to lord it over
her social inferiors. Now the boss is coming to dinner. The
evening will be a success or failure, comedy or tragedy,
depending upon the scriptwriter's imperatives; the protago-
nists will enjoy, lose, or find illusory the rewards of ambition. Is not some such recurring human predicament to be
found, again enormously magnified, at the core of *Macbeth*? The middle-level executive has become a brave general. His wife is ambitious. The boss is not only his guest
but also his king and kinsman. Promotion, it seems, can be
achieved only by murder. The Macbeths' castle becomes an
emblem of hell. Good digestion and sleep go by the boards.
The everyday in *Macbeth* is pushed, with fierce poetic and
dramatic concentration, to a tragic ultimate. But the essential human substance remains a constant.

Or take *King Lear*. It is not my game tonight to gainsay
the vastness of Shakespeare's design, at once awesomely
cosmic and finitely human, or the intensity with which that
design is executed. Again and again, critics marvel at the
intensity. "So powerful is the current of the poet's imagination," Dr. Johnson wrote, "that the mind, which once ven-
tures within it, is hurried irresistibly along. . . ." In a celebrated passage of his correspondence John Keats observed:
"The excellence of every art is its intensity, capable of making all disagreeables evaporate, from their being in close
relationship with Beauty and Truth. Examine *King Lear*,
and you will find this exemplified throughout." When that
storm breaks on the heath, none of us—spectators or readers—can scramble for cover. I have sometimes toyed with
the notion that in Elizabethan tragedy all roads lead to *Lear*.
But that is the subject for another evening and another lecture. My concern now is not with the grandeur of the play
but with its irreducible human substance, not with its poetry
but with the prose of its dilemmas.

King Lear is Shakespeare's play about retirement. We all

know, from our elders or from approaching that stage ourselves, what problems are presented by letting go. At the same time that we give up, we want to hold on. Then there are the children. More often than not, we have already given them up to matrimony and therefore to leading their own lives. Now if, after retirement, we decide to live with them—an extreme solution—or to spend long periods under their roofs, such arrangements can present problems. How will the children accept the domestic burden of the visit? And how will thcy mcasurc up to parental expectation? Somewhere down the pike after retirement awaits death, and for many that is an inevitability too fearful to contemplate. It is all in *Lear*. The protagonist has reached that stage of life's journey when he must (as Freud puts it) "renounce love, choose death, and make friends with the necessity of dying." This is ordinary; but of course Lear is very special. The job he is vacating is the kingship, and the children whose affections mean so much to him are either monstrously cruel or capable of redemptive love.

Separated from Shakespeare's transfiguring genius and reduced to bedrock, *Lear* is everywhere around us. My point is that the play owes much to the bedrock, just as it owes so much to the genius. Let me remind you of one recent version. Many of you have, I expect, seen Paul Mazursky's film *Harry and Tonto*, released six years ago to friendly notices and widespread popular acclaim. Art Carney won the Academy Award for best actor that year for his portrayal of Harry Combs, a seventy-two-year-old New York widower and retired high-school teacher who is forcibly evicted from his Upper West Side apartment building, which is scheduled for demolition. Harry embarks on a long odyssey which takes him to his three children—a son in New Jersey, a daughter in Chicago, another son in Los Angeles. Accompanying him is Tonto, a large ginger cat. The encounters with family prove in various ways unsatisfactory. Harry ends up alone in Santa Monica, wiser in a stoical sort of way, watching the surf break upon the glistening beach and children playing in the sand. It isn't Shakespeare.

Or isn't it? I have talked with colleagues who have a special interest in Shakcspcarc and film, or Shakespeare on film, and I must confess that they haven't seen Harry and Tonto as Mazursky's *Lear*. After all, the arts are filled with accidental parallels, just as life is, and for the critic, armed with his leveling bulldozer, these pose problems. But I am right about *Harry and Tonto*. To validate interpretation, and in anticipation of my address tonight, I managed to put my hands on the novelization of the script, by Mazursky and Josh Greenfeld, published in the same year that the movie was exhibited. Here is Harry being carried out of the house in his easy chair (I have not tampered with small lapses in his quotations):

> The crowd roared when they saw Harry and Tonto, perched on the rocker, as if it were a palanquin, being carried out of the building by two grunting cops.
>
> '"Blow, winds, and crack your cheeks! Rage! Blow!"' they heard Harry bellowing.
>
> 'Pop!' Burt called out.
>
> '"You cataracts and hurricanes, spout till you have drench'd our steeples, drown'd the cocks!"'
>
> 'Drown the cocks! Drown the cocks!' echoed a teenager.
>
> 'Pop!' Burt implored. 'Act your age!'
>
> 'I am,' said Harry, and resumed his histrionic raging:
>
>> You sulphurous and thought-executing fires
>> Vaunt-couriers of oak-cleaving thunderbolts,
>> Singe my white head!
>
> 'You tell him, man!' someone shouted.

Later, when he is with his son Burt, these exchanges take place:

> 'You were thinking about Lear.'
>
> 'Lear who?'
>
> 'I don't know.'
>
> 'King Lear!' Harry exploded. 'He gave up his real estate, too. And what did they do to him? They foreclosed. That's life. . . .'

In Chicago, with his daughter Shirley, four times married but still childless, he is visibly upset:

> 'You'll never have kids,' he breathed out.
>
> 'I doubt it,' said Shirley.

'"I loved her most and thought to set my rest on her kind nursery,"' Harry quoted.

'Sorry, Harry,' Shirley said sharply, 'I spent eighteen years listening to Shakespeare.'

Harry exploded. 'What's wrong with Shakespeare? He was the greatest writer this world will ever know.'

Shirley smiled 'But he wasn't my father.'

Harry gave up. 'I'm tired,' he said.

Tonto, the cat, is Mazursky's equivalent to Shakespeare's Fool. His presence and companionship, however limited by his feline status, enable Harry to express what would otherwise go unverbalized. The Fool disappears from *Lear*, although Shakespeare does not tell us what has happened to him. At around the same point in the film Tonto dies.

It is curious that the movie's antecedents went mostly unnoticed by well-informed viewers, but that merely testifies to the skill of the translation and the universal accessibility of the dramatic material. Which is the point I have been making. *Harry and Tonto* is not filmed tragedy but picaresque domestic drama which skates on the thin ice of sentimentality and sometimes falls through but never wallows in maudlin emotion. *King Lear* achieves heights to which Mazursky's modest film sensibly never aspires. But the human predicaments underlying both share points of reference.

Superior genius and bourgeois ordinariness make not so strange bedfellows. It is astonishing that anybody could have written *Macbeth* and *Lear* and the rest, but not, per se, that they should have been written by a son of Stratford who married young, fathered three children, became the grandest box-office success of his age (afterwards of any age), and retired to the town of his birth, where—according to an early biographer—he spent his last days "as all Men of Good Sense will wish theirs may be, in Ease, Retirement, and the Conversation of his Friends."[1]

---

1. I have not revised this paper to reduce its essentially oral character; nor furnished documentation of sources which are self-evident.